THE
FOUNDATIONS
OF
TRUE FAITH

Ernest Addo

Copyright © 2015 Ernest Addo

Published by Little Books Publications, United Kingdom

First edition 2015

Email Ernest Addo:

ernest.addo1@yahoo.com

Find out more about Ernest Addo at:

www.facebook.com/LivingJesusTabernacle

ISBN: 978-0-9932250-1-7

Printed by Polestar UK Print Limited (Wheatons)

Dedication

I dedicate this book to my wife Angella Addo.

Angie, you have been with me through thick and thin. Thank you for your steadfast love and support in the ministry and life as a whole.

May God bless you and may He continue to use you mightily.

Acknowledgements

I would like to thank Evette Scott for her
tireless effort in editing the books and for
availing herself for the ministry.
You will never lose your blessing.

I would also like to thank Mrs Dionne Thomas
for her constant encouragement and support.
May God bless you abundantly.

Contents

Preface

Everyone has Faith

Every human being is on a search for something to satisfy their soul. No matter how wealthy a person is, there is still that emptiness within their soul. In our search we try so many things; from sex, alcohol, drugs, money, cars, houses, academia, fame to even the worship of objects carved by the hands of men. Sadly, many have ended up on the path to destruction through their fruitless attempts to satisfy this need. The truth is, this void cannot be filled with worldly things. It can only be filled by the divine power of God.

We know there is something greater that can satisfy the longing of our souls. Yet many people fail to recognise this 'something greater' as an Almighty God. Instead, people attribute this 'something greater' to philosophies or other beliefs. In recent times, people are depositing all their faith and trust in science. But science is limited. Science bases its findings on something that already exists. How can mankind put its faith and trust in things created instead of the Creator? It is irrational. It rather makes more sense to trust in the One who created science. We cannot trust in science more than the Being through whom the universe came into existence.

God is not a theory, God is not money and God is certainly not a statue with many hands, heads, mouths and legs. God cannot be fed by man. In fact I will say it again, God is not a statue. He is not hiding in an obscure place for people to come and worship. He has neither beginning nor ending because He himself is existence!

The Christian faith is different in that we put our faith and trust in a living God. *His name is Jesus, the Lord God Almighty. He is True Faith!*

That is why I am writing this book on THE FOUNDATIONS OF TRUE FAITH so that you can learn about true faith and channel your faith in the right direction.

Section I

࿖

What is Faith?

Their idols are silver and gold, the work of men's hands. They have mouths, but they speak not: eyes have they, but they see not: They have ears, but they hear not: noses have they, but they smell not: They have hands, but they handle not: feet have they, but they walk not: neither speak they through their throat. They that make them are like unto them; so is every one that trusteth in them.

Psalm 115:4-8

Chapter 1

What do you Worship?

Wat you choose to worship as your god is very significant. I once watched a clip of a lady who said she had to memorise the names of over 2,000 gods. What an incredible number of different gods catering for different needs! I am grateful I have one Almighty, All-Sufficient God who is exceedingly, abundantly able to do more than I could ask or ever hope for.

I once spoke to a lady who informed me that she fed her god every morning. I then asked, "where is your god?" She replied, "in my small room". So I asked "how can your god live in just a small part of your house and why do you feed your god instead of him feeding you?" This lady could not give me an answer. You see, my God feeds me and provides for all my needs.

One day, I saw a god displayed in a man's car. I wondered, "how can you carry your god around?" "Surely, your god is supposed to carry you and not the other way round?" My mighty God protects me and bears me in His everlasting arms.

Amazingly, none of these gods produced an answer for their followers. Yet you see millions of people, both educated and uneducated, wasting their time worshipping objects carved by men. These objects are kept in shrines, homes and even cars for people to carry around and worship them.

God is NOT an Object made with Hands

Millions of people worship objects made of gold, silver, stone and even wood. They carve these objects into shapes and bow down to things that they have made with their own hands. These objects have eyes yet cannot see. They have ears yet cannot hear. They have mouths yet cannot speak. They have noses yet cannot smell. They have arms yet cannot lift. They even have legs yet they cannot walk. Instead, it is the very people who worship these so-called gods or idols who perform these activities for their god. In short, these are deaf and dumb idols.

My Bishop once told a story about one of his pastors who went to visit a village. Whilst he was approaching the village, he suddenly realised he needed to urinate. He saw an area just off the footpath, by a large stone, and decided that was a suitable spot. As he started, he heard a loud commotion. Alarmed, he looked up and saw a crowd approaching him and shouting; "stop urinating on our god, stop urinating on our god!" The large stone was the god of the villagers. This god is an example of a deaf and dumb idol. It could not speak for itself, even just to tell the pastor to stop urinating on him. It was totally silent.

The word of God describes these deaf and dumb idols in the following passage of scriptures:

Their idols are silver and gold, the work of men's hands.

They have mouths, but they speak not: eyes have they, but they see not:

They have ears, but they hear not: noses have they, but they smell not:

They have hands, but they handle not: feet have they, but they walk not: neither speak they through their throat.

They that make them are like unto them; so is every one that trusteth in them.

Psalm 115:4-8

Hear ye the word which the LORD speaketh unto you, O house of Israel: Thus saith the LORD, Learn not the way of the heathen, and be not dismayed at the signs of heaven; for the heathen are dismayed at them.

For the customs of the people are vain: for one cutteth a tree out of the forest, the work of the hands of the workman, with the axe. They deck it with silver and with gold; they fasten it with nails and with hammers, that it move not. They are upright as the palm tree, but speak not: they must needs be borne, because they cannot go.

Be not afraid of them; for they cannot do evil, neither also is it in them to do good. Forasmuch as there is none like unto thee, O LORD; thou art great, and thy name is great in might. Who would not fear thee, O King of nations? for to thee doth it appertain: forasmuch as among all the wise men of the nations, and in all their kingdoms, there is none like unto thee.

But they are altogether brutish and foolish: the stock is a doctrine of vanities. Silver spread into plates is brought from Tarshish, and gold from Uphaz, the work of the workman, and of the hands of the founder: blue and purple is their clothing: they are all the work of cunning men.

But the LORD is the true God, he is the living God, and an everlasting king: at his wrath the earth shall tremble, and the nations shall not be able to abide his indignation. Thus shall ye say unto them, The gods that have not made the heavens and the earth, even they shall perish from the earth, and from under these heavens.

Jeremiah 10:1-11

What profiteth the graven image that the maker thereof hath graven it; the molten image, and a teacher of lies, that the maker of his work trusteth therein, to make dumb idols?

Woe unto him that saith to the wood, Awake; to the dumb stone, Arise, it shall teach! Behold, it is laid over with gold and silver, and there is no breath at all in the midst of it.

Habakkuk 2:18-19

God is NOT an Animal

Some religions consider animals as god and they bow down to these animals which were created for us to eat. God the Creator of the heavens and the earth is not an animal. How can a human being created in the very image of the Most High God bow down to animals that God has given man dominion over? How can creatures such as cows, snakes, pigs, tigers, elephants, monkeys, wolves, dogs, goats, horses etc. be worshipped in His place?

And God said, Let us make man in our image, after our likeness: and let them have dominion over the fish of the sea, and over the fowl of the air, and over the cattle, and over all the earth, and over every creeping thing that creepeth upon the earth.

Genesis 1:26

The Almighty God created human beings to be superior to animals. To see humans worshipping animals means mankind has indeed lowered itself and made animals more superior than themselves. God put mankind in charge of animals, not the other way round. This is ignorance to the fullest extent. Mankind has reached this state because they have refused to recognise the Creator of the heavens and the earth as God. The verse of scripture below explains it all.

Because that, when they knew God, they glorified him not as God, neither were thankful; but became vain in their imaginations, and their foolish heart was darkened.

Professing themselves to be wise, they became fools, And changed the glory of the uncorruptible God into an image made like to corruptible man, and to birds, and fourfooted beasts, and creeping things.

Romans 1:21-23

A darkened heart and mind is hostile to God and such a person will serve anything, regardless of whether they are educated or illiterate.

God is NOT a Man

Some religions actually worship men and this is not right. When you worship a man, that man becomes your idol. We must understand that God is not an imperfect human being, neither is He an icon or a figurehead. The Bible tells us that God is not a man and God cannot lie.

God is not a man, that he should lie; neither the son of man, that he should repent: hath he said, and shall he not do it? or hath he spoken, and shall he not make it good?

Numbers 23:19

Men lie all the time. We cannot even take care of ourselves, let alone be worshipped as god. Men change all the time but God can never change. A man will say to a lady "I love you and I want to marry you" and later change his mind and break that lady's heart. How can such a person who is not morally correct be your god? It is simple, a man cannot be your god!

In fact, one of the main reasons why a man cannot be your god is that he does not even know when he will die. Today he is alive but tomorrow he is dead. **Job 14** explains that even a tree has more hope than a man because it can regrow after being cut down.

Man that is born of a woman is of few days, and full of trouble. He cometh forth like a flower, and is cut down: he fleeth also as a shadow, and continueth not. And dost thou open thine eyes upon such an one, and bringest me into judgment with thee? Who can bring a clean thing out of an unclean? not one.

Seeing his days are determined, the number of his months are with thee, thou hast appointed his bounds that he cannot pass; Turn from him, that he may rest, till he shall accomplish, as an hireling, his day.

For there is hope of a tree, if it be cut down, that it will sprout again, and that the tender branch thereof will not cease. Though the root thereof wax old in the earth, and the stock thereof die in the ground; Yet through the scent of water it will bud, and bring forth boughs like a plant.

But man dieth, and wasteth away: yea, man giveth up the ghost, and where is he?

Job 14:1-10

God is a Spirit

Do not be deceived by the many definitions men have given to God! Many have perceived the Creator to be a man, an animal, a stone and even trees. But these definitions are completely wrong. God is none of these helpless, inferior things. The word of God gives a classic definition of God. Almighty God is a Spirit.

God is a Spirit: and they that worship him must worship him in spirit and in truth.

John 4:24

The above passage of scripture in **John 4:24** puts God in the right perspective. God is a Spirit. He neither has beginning nor end. He Himself is the beginning and the end. No one created God because

He Himself is existence. He cannot be compared to any kind of god. **There is only one God and beside Him there is no other god.** All others are liars. Any human being who claim to be Almighty God is a liar.

Unto thee it was shewed, that thou mightest know that the LORD he is God; there is none else beside him.

Deuteronomy 4:35

Now faith is the substance of things hoped for, the evidence of things not seen.

Hebrews 11:1

Chapter 2

Revelation of Faith

Most Christians tend to refer to the opening scripture in **Hebrews 11** when they speak of faith. This scripture tells us *what* faith is. But I am going to share with you a deeper revelation of faith, from this very same scripture, of *who* faith is. The word "Substance" used in **Hebrews 11:1**, comes from the Greek word "Hupostasis".

> **Now faith is the SUBSTANCE of things hoped for, the evidence of things not seen.**
>
> **Hebrews 11:1**

In Greek, "Hupostasis" is interpreted to mean *a person*. Let's take a look at **Hebrews 1:3.**

> **Who being the brightness of his glory, and the express image of his PERSON, and upholding all things by the word of his power, when he had by himself purged our sins, sat down on the right hand of the Majesty on high;**
>
> **Hebrews 1:3**

The word "Person" used in **Hebrews 1:3** also comes from the same Greek word "Hupostasis". Therefore, the word "Person" used in **Hebrews 1:3** has the same meaning as the word "Substance" in **Hebrews 11:1**. This is a profound revelation of faith! Both scriptures tell us that the Greek word "Hupostasis" is a *person*. So, who is this person that these scriptures are describing? Who are they revealing?

John 1 tells us that the Word, which was God, became flesh and dwelt amongst men. **That is, the Word became a person!** The scriptures in **Hebrews** are certainly talking about Jesus who came down to the earth in the form of a person! There is no other god who has done this. Only Jesus Christ alone! This is an astonishing revelation!

In the beginning was the Word, and the Word was with God, and the Word was God.

John 1:1

And the Word was made flesh, and dwelt among us, (and we beheld his glory, the glory as of the only begotten of the Father,) full of grace and truth.

John 1:14

It is undisputable, faith IS Jesus Christ!

Let's look again at **Hebrews 11:1**. Now we know that faith is Jesus Christ, the scripture has become even clearer!

Now faith is the substance of things hoped for, the evidence of things not seen.

Hebrews 11:1

Therefore JESUS is the substance of things hoped for and JESUS is the evidence of things not seen. It truly gives us the real definition of faith! Jesus is faith Himself and not just any kind of god that people are following. The word of God states that Jesus is the beginning of faith and He is the end of faith. Before Him there is no faith and after Him there is no faith.

LOOKING UNTO JESUS THE AUTHOR AND FINISHER OF OUR FAITH; who for the joy that was set before him endured the cross, despising the shame, and is set down at the right hand of the throne of God.

Hebrews 12:2

And without controversy great is the mystery of godliness: God was manifest in the flesh, justified in the Spirit, seen of angels, preached unto the Gentiles, believed on in the world, received up into glory.

1 Timothy 3:16

Chapter 3

Jesus is God

Most people, and indeed most religions, do not accept Jesus as God. They think He is a human being just like us. The most common argument is, how can a person who had a natural birth like us be God? Tighten your seat belt because I am going to prove to you beyond doubt that Jesus Christ is God! In fact, not only is Jesus God Himself, He is also the real faith that people are searching for.

The name "Jesus" comes from the Hebrew word "Yehoshua" meaning *Saviour* or *God who is salvation*.

And she shall bring forth a son, and thou shalt call his name JESUS: for he shall save his people from their sins.
Matthew 1:21

Another name for Jesus is "Emmanuel", which comes from the Greek word "Emmanouel", which is interpreted as *God with us*.

Behold, a virgin shall be with child, and shall bring forth a son, and they shall call his name EMMANUEL, which being interpreted is, God with us.
Matthew 1:23

The word of God also refers to Jesus as the express image of God in **Hebrews 1:3**. The phrase "express image" means: *the exact copy or a representation, a stamped copy, engraved copy, to look exactly the same*. Jesus is the express image of God the Father.

Who being the brightness of his glory, and THE EXPRESS IMAGE OF HIS PERSON, and upholding all things by the word of his power, when he had by himself purged our sins, sat down on the right hand of the Majesty on high;

Hebrews 1:3

Philip, one of the disciples asked the Lord to show him God the Father. Just like Philip, there are believers, denominations and churches who are still confused about how Jesus is God and also the Son of God. Some even say that they will worship only God the Father because Jesus is the Son of God whilst God is God. This is absolute nonsense because Jesus Himself IS God. Like Philip, they want to see the Father before they can believe in Jesus.

Philip saith unto him, Lord, shew us the Father, and it sufficeth us.

John 14:8

But Jesus gave Philip a very profound answer which is an eye opener and settles the confusion as to whether He is God or not.

Jesus saith unto him, Have I been so long time with you, and yet hast thou not known me, Philip? HE THAT HATH SEEN ME HATH SEEN THE FATHER; and how sayest thou then, Shew us the Father?

John 14:9

Jesus is God. He is referred to as the Mighty God in **Isaiah 9:6**. He is the great God and our Saviour. In the scripture below, God the Father is referring to Jesus as God.

But unto the Son he saith, Thy throne, O God, is for ever and ever; a sceptre of righteousness is the sceptre of thy kingdom.
Hebrews 1:8

Jesus Christ is the Word of the living God and the word itself is God.

In the beginning was the Word, and the Word was with God, and the Word was God. The same was in the beginning with God.
John 1:1-2

Now in same chapter of John, in verse 14, the Bible tells us that the word became flesh and dwelt among us. This is the greatest miracle that ever happened in the history of the earth. God became a man.

And the Word was made flesh, and dwelt among us, (and we beheld his glory, the glory as of the only begotten of the Father,) full of grace and truth.
John 1:14

This scripture in **1 Timothy** seals it all.

And without controversy great is the mystery of godliness: God was manifest in the flesh, justified in the Spirit, seen of angels, preached unto the Gentiles, believed on in the world, received up into glory.
1 Timothy 3:16

This verse is saying that without argument or further proof, God was manifested in the flesh. It seals it all! Hallelujah!

Christianity does not teach that we have three separate gods. We have one God: God the Father, God the Son, God the Holy Spirit. The word of God says that the fullness of the Godhead dwells in Jesus. We can never truly comprehend the trinity of the Godhead because we are very limited in our thinking and our human minds cannot completely understand it.

For in him dwelleth all the fulness of the Godhead bodily.
Colossians 2:9

The secret things belong unto the LORD our God: but those things which are revealed belong unto us and to our children for ever, that we may do all the words of this law.
Deuteronomy 29:29

The LORD possessed me in the beginning of his way, before his works of old. I was set up from everlasting, from the beginning, or ever the earth was.

When there were no depths, I was brought forth; when there were no fountains abounding with water.

Before the mountains were settled, before the hills was I brought forth:

While as yet he had not made the earth, nor the fields, nor the highest part of the dust of the world. When he prepared the heavens, I was there: when he set a compass upon the face of the depth:

When he established the clouds above: when he strengthened the fountains of the deep: When he gave to the sea his decree, that the waters should not pass his commandment: when he appointed the foundations of the earth:

Then I was by him, as one brought up with him: and I was daily his delight, rejoicing always before him;

Rejoicing in the habitable part of his earth; and my delights were with the sons of men.

Proverbs 8:22-31

Chapter 4

The Pre-Existent Jesus

Jesus existed with God the Father and God the Holy Spirit before the foundation of this world. He neither has a beginning nor an ending. In **Genesis 1:26**, the Bible tells us that God said, "*let us make man in our own image*". In this scripture, we can see that the word "us" is used in place of the pronoun "we". For example, when you are talking about a group of people you can say, "They took **us** to the market". So, if "us" is referring to a group, then this scripture is certainly referring to God the Father, God the Son and God the Holy Spirit. These three are one and the same.

And God said, Let US make man in our image, after our likeness: and let them have dominion over the fish of the sea, and over the fowl of the air, and over the cattle, and over all the earth, and over every creeping thing that creepeth upon the earth.

Genesis 1:26

In another verse, in **Genesis 3:22**, God says "*man is become as one of us*".

And the LORD God said, Behold, the man is become as one of US, to know good and evil: and now, lest he put forth his hand, and take also of the tree of life, and eat, and live for ever:

Genesis 3:22

Again, in **Genesis 11:7**, God says *"let us go down"*.

Go to, let US go down, and there confound their language, that they may not understand one another's speech.

Genesis 11:7

God Almighty always made mention of the trinity. He never referred to Himself alone. Jesus has been the God of ages and Himself is God Almighty. Jesus existed in the beginning with God. He existed before all things and by Him all things exist. Jesus is the Alpha and Omega, the Beginning and the End. He is the First and the Last! Hallelujah!

Here is an amazing passage of scripture from **Proverbs** that reveals the fact that Jesus existed in the beginning and before the world was ever created.

The LORD possessed me in the beginning of his way, before his works of old.

I was set up from everlasting, from the beginning, or ever the earth was.

When there were no depths, I was brought forth; when there were no fountains abounding with water.

Before the mountains were settled, before the hills was I brought forth:

While as yet he had not made the earth, nor the fields, nor the highest part of the dust of the world.

When he prepared the heavens, I was there: when he set a compass upon the face of the depth:

When he established the clouds above: when he strengthened the fountains of the deep:

When he gave to the sea his decree, that the waters should not pass his commandment: when he appointed the foundations of the earth:

Then I was by him, as one brought up with him: and I was daily his delight, rejoicing always before him;

Rejoicing in the habitable part of his earth; and my delights were with the sons of men.

Proverbs 8:22-31

Let this mind be in you, which was also in Christ Jesus:
Who, being in the form of God, thought it not robbery to be equal with God:
But made himself of no reputation, and took upon him the form of a servant, and was made in the likeness of men:
And being found in fashion as a man, he humbled himself, and became obedient unto death, even the death of the cross.

Philippians 2:5-8

Chapter 5

God Became a Man

The greatest miracle in the history of mankind is that our Creator became like one of us and walked right on this earth. The Lord Jesus who is a Spirit was transformed by the Holy Spirit and given a body to become like one of us. This is extraordinary!

Wherefore when he cometh into the world, he saith, Sacrifice and offering thou wouldest not, but a body hast thou prepared me:

Hebrews 10:5

And the Word was made flesh, and dwelt among us, (and we beheld his glory, the glory as of the only begotten of the Father,) full of grace and truth.

John 1:14

Philippians 2 reveals that the Lord Jesus disrobed Himself of His heavenly nature to take upon Himself the form and the nature of man. This is a mystery that cannot be easily explained.

Who, being in the form of God, thought it not robbery to be equal with God:

But made himself of no reputation, and took upon him the form of a servant, and was made in the likeness of men:

And being found in fashion as a man, he humbled himself, and became obedient unto death, even the death of the cross.

Philippians 2:6-8

This profound truth has been misunderstood by many. It is truly incomprehensible to the natural human mind and cannot be understood. It can only be discerned spiritually.

But the natural man receiveth not the things of the Spirit of God: for they are foolishness unto him: neither can he know them, because they are spiritually discerned.

1 Corinthians 2:14

Pastor Benny Hinn once shared the following illustration used by the evangelist Billy Graham. I think this illustration explains superbly how Lord Jesus disrobed Himself for our sakes.

"If you were God and you created an ant and you realised that the ant was walking into fire, how would you stop the ant from walking into the fire? The ant does not have your form or nature and cannot understand your language. Your voice will sound like thunder when you speak to that little ant and for that matter you will rather scare the ant into the fire. In order to save the ant, you have to become like the ant so that the ant can understand when you tell it that you are walking into the fire."

Take note. This is *precisely* what God did for us. He became like men so He could relate to us, speak to us and change the course of our lives forever.

For we have not an high priest which cannot be touched with the feeling of our infirmities; but was in all points tempted like as we are, yet without sin.

Hebrews 4:15

Man was heading towards hell with no hope. Satan had corrupted the human race with sin and we needed to be freed from the bondage of sin. God in His mercy, became a man and offered us the gospel of salvation so that as many as believe in Him are turned away from hell fire.

He that committeth sin is of the devil; for the devil sinneth from the beginning. For this purpose the Son of God was manifested, that he might destroy the works of the devil.

1 John 3:8

And without controversy great is the mystery of godliness: God was manifest in the flesh, justified in the Spirit, seen of angels, preached unto the Gentiles, believed on in the world, received up into glory.

1 Timothy 3:16

Let this mind be in you, which was also in Christ Jesus: Who, being in the form of God, thought it not robbery to be equal with God:

But made himself of no reputation, and took upon him the form of a servant, and was made in the likeness of men:

And being found in fashion as a man, he humbled himself, and became obedient unto death, even the death of the cross.

Philippians 2:5-8

Section II

❧❧

Faith Facts

But without faith it is impossible to please him: for he that cometh to God must believe that he is, and that he is a rewarder of them that diligently seek him.

Hebrews 11:6

Chapter 6

The Necessity of Faith

It is impossible for a person to be saved without faith. In other words, it is impossible to be saved without Jesus. Looking at the scripture below carefully, you will notice that we are only saved through faith in Jesus. The grace of God is available for salvation but only those who reach out to Jesus shall be saved. Salvation through faith means salvation through Jesus.

You Cannot be Saved without Faith

For by grace are ye saved THROUGH FAITH; and that not of yourselves: it is the gift of God: Not of works, lest any man should boast.

Ephesians 2:8-9

And, behold, a woman in the city, which was a sinner, when she knew that Jesus sat at meat in the Pharisee's house, brought an alabaster box of ointment, And stood at his feet behind him weeping, and began to wash his feet with tears, and did wipe them with the hairs of her head, and kissed his feet, and anointed them with the ointment.

Now when the Pharisee which had bidden him saw it, he spake within himself, saying, This man, if he were a prophet, would have known who and what manner of woman this is that toucheth him: for she is a sinner.

And Jesus answering said unto him, Simon, I have somewhat to say unto thee. And he saith, Master, say on. There was a certain creditor which had two debtors: the one owed five hundred pence, and the other fifty. And when they had nothing to pay, he frankly forgave them both. Tell me therefore, which of them will love him most? Simon answered and said, I suppose that he, to whom he forgave most. And he said unto him, Thou hast rightly judged.

And he turned to the woman, and said unto Simon, Seest thou this woman? I entered into thine house, thou gavest me no water for my feet: but she hath washed my feet with tears, and wiped them with the hairs of her head. Thou gavest me no kiss: but this woman since the time I came in hath not ceased to kiss my feet. My head with oil thou didst not anoint: but this woman hath anointed my feet with ointment.

Wherefore I say unto thee, Her sins, which are many, are forgiven; for she loved much: but to whom little is forgiven, the same loveth little.

And he said unto her, Thy sins are forgiven. And they that sat at meat with him began to say within themselves, Who is this that forgiveth sins also? And he said to the woman, THY FAITH HATH SAVED THEE; go in peace.

Luke 7:37-50

There is no other way to salvation; you cannot be saved by your own works or self efforts. You cannot be saved through any other name or means. It is only through Jesus.

You can love everybody, you can be very kind, you can give all your money to the poor, you can establish many charities to help mankind, you can pay your tithes, sing in the choir and even preach but none of these can save you. The truth is that you cannot be saved by your own works. In fact, all our good deeds are like filthy rags before the Lord.

I often hear people say, "I am a good person and therefore I will go to heaven". There is no such thing as you are too good to go hell. Do not be deceived, you can never be good enough for heaven. It is not by our own works but by the mercy and salvation of God alone. There is only one way to get saved and that is through Jesus Christ. **John 10:7** tells us that even the very door to heaven is Jesus.

Jesus said, *"I am the way, the truth and the life, no man comes to the father but by Me" (John 14:6)*. All others are liars. My friend, do not be fooled by the doctrine of devils being preached by some people because one day they will all bow before the King of kings and the Lord of lords.

The word of God also tells us in **Acts 4:12** that there is no other name under heaven by which we can be saved. In other words, there is no salvation in any other name except Jesus. If you put your trust in other things you perceive as god, then you may be very disappointed at the end of life. Many have called for a priest to pray for them whilst lying on their deathbed. That is when they see the reality of the spiritual world as they can see the demons coming to drag their soul to hell. That is when they realise that they have lived a life of lies serving false gods. They call for a priest to pray for them but it is in vain. At that point it will be too late. Put your faith and trust in Jesus today and receive true salvation. You shall not be disappointed at the end of life!

You Cannot Please God without Faith

The word "Please" means to *satisfy* or *to be content*. You cannot please or satisfy God without faith. In other words, it is impossible to please God without Jesus. Jesus is the reason why we have access to God. His blood is what makes us holy and acceptable before God and we cannot do without Him. He Himself is Faith and the Bible says it is impossible to please God without Faith.

But WITHOUT FAITH IT IS IMPOSSIBLE TO PLEASE HIM: for he that cometh to God must believe that he is, and that he is a rewarder of them that diligently seek him.
Hebrews 11:6

The word "Please" used in this scripture from **Hebrews 11**, is the Greek word "Euraesteo" which means; *to gratify entirely* or *to make happy*. Making God happy is a substantial task. You wonder, how can a human being full of infirmities make God happy? The majority of Christians live in sin even after salvation. Christians lie, steal, fornicate, commit adultery, gossip, worship idols and all sorts of other sins. For some, it is almost impossible to live the new life they have found in Jesus.

So pleasing God certainly cannot be achieved through human efforts or deeds. It is the entire work of Jesus. As a Christian, we can only please or make God happy when He looks at us and sees us washed in the precious blood of Jesus.

And from Jesus Christ, who is the faithful witness, and the first begotten of the dead, and the prince of the kings of the earth. Unto him that loved us, and washed us from our sins in his own blood,

Revelation 1:5

You Cannot be Justified without Faith

Therefore being JUSTIFIED BY FAITH, we have peace with God through our Lord Jesus Christ:

Romans 5:1

Therefore we conclude that a man is JUSTIFIED BY FAITH without the deeds of the law.

Romans 3:28

Therefore as by the offence of one judgment came upon all men to condemnation; even so by the righteousness of one the free gift came upon all men unto JUSTIFICATION of life.

Romans 5:18

The word "Justification" in the above scripture comes from the Greek word "Dikaioo" which means; *to be declared righteous* or *not guilty, innocent and free*. A born again Christian is a guiltless Christian. Many are still haunted by their past sins because they have not accepted this truth. When you receive Jesus, all your sins are forgiven and you are now a new person. The moment you received the

Lord into your heart, at the same instant, you are cleared of all sins. In other words you are justified the minute you become born again and repent of your sins.

Jesus told an example of two men who went to pray. One was repentant of his sins and the other boasted of his good deeds. The one who repented of his sins was justified.

Two men went up into the temple to pray; the one a Pharisee, and the other a publican.

The Pharisee stood and prayed thus with himself, God, I thank thee, that I am not as other men are, extortioners, unjust, adulterers, or even as this publican. I fast twice in the week, I give tithes of all that I possess.

And the publican, standing afar off, would not lift up so much as his eyes unto heaven, but smote upon his breast, saying, God be merciful to me a sinner.

I tell you, this man went down to his house justified rather than the other: for every one that exalteth himself shall be abased; and he that humbleth himself shall be exalted.

Luke 18:10-14

The scripture reveals it clearly, you cannot be justified without faith in Jesus. Jesus is the reason why we can have fellowship with the Father. Without Jesus, none of us will be guiltless because nothing can wash away our sins except His blood. This is exactly what Apostle Paul told the people of Antioch. We are justified through Jesus alone.

Be it known unto you therefore, men and brethren, that through this man is preached unto you the forgiveness of sins:

And by him all that believe are justified from all things, from which ye could not be justified by the law of Moses.

Act 13:38-39

You Cannot have Access to the Father without Faith

It is amazing that we can have sweet fellowship with the Father. This has been made possible by the Lord Jesus who Himself is Faith. Without Jesus, we cannot go to the Father. Glory be to the Lord that by the sacrifice of the Lamb of God we His children have the right to enter into His presence!

By whom also we have ACCESS by faith into this grace wherein we stand, and rejoice in hope of the glory of God.

Romans 5:2

In whom we have boldness and ACCESS with confidence by the faith of him.

Ephesians 3:12

The word "Access" in these scriptures is the Greek word "Prosagoge" which means; *admission, right to enter* and the *right to approach*. Which means through Faith, or through Jesus, we have the right to approach God and we also have the right to enter into His presence.

You Cannot Live without Faith

Now the just shall LIVE BY FAITH: but if any man draw back, my soul shall have no pleasure in him.

Hebrews 10:38

Behold, his soul which is lifted up is not upright in him: but THE JUST SHALL LIVE BY HIS FAITH.

Habakkuk 2:4

For therein is the righteousness of God revealed from faith to faith: as it is written, THE JUST SHALL LIVE BY FAITH.

Romans 1:17

But that no man is justified by the law in the sight of God, it is evident: for, THE JUST SHALL LIVE BY FAITH.

Galatians 3:11

We cannot live without faith. A songwriter once wrote, "Because He lives, I can face tomorrow". There are so many troubles and evil in this world. You cannot survive on this earth without the Creator Himself. It can get so difficult that people commit suicide because they think there is no more hope left for them. But I say to you, Christ in us is the hope of glory. Apostle Paul knew this fact. That is why he wrote to the Galatians and said;

I am crucified with Christ: nevertheless I live; yet not I, but Christ liveth in me: and the life which I now live in the flesh I LIVE BY THE FAITH OF THE SON OF GOD, who loved me, and gave himself for me.

Galatians 2:20

We live, move and have our very existence through Jesus Christ.

For in him we live, and move, and have our being; as certain also of your own poets have said, For we are also his offspring.

Acts 17:28

You Cannot Walk as a Christian without Faith

The word "Walk" is the Greek word "Peripateo" which translated means *to live* or *to follow*.

FOR WE WALK BY FAITH, not by sight:

2 Corinthians 5:7

To be a Christian means to live and follow the steps of Jesus. Jesus lived a life of faith. He was not moved by what He saw around Him or the circumstances that hindered Him. He operated and lived a life of faith. In **Mark 11**, Jesus was passing by a fig tree and wanted to eat some figs as He was hungry. The fig tree was not ready to bear fruit but Jesus demonstrated the power of faith.

And Jesus entered into Jerusalem, and into the temple: and when he had looked round about upon all things, and now the eventide was come, he went out unto Bethany with the twelve.

And on the morrow, when they were come from Bethany, he was hungry: And seeing a fig tree afar off having leaves, he came, if haply he might find any thing thereon: and when he came to it, he found nothing but leaves; for the time of figs was not yet.

And Jesus answered and said unto it, No man eat fruit of thee hereafter for ever. And his disciples heard it.

Mark 11:11-14

After Jesus had spoken these words of faith, the fig tree began to wither just as He had said.

And in the morning, as they passed by, they saw the fig tree dried up from the roots.

And Peter calling to remembrance saith unto him, Master, behold, the fig tree which thou cursedst is withered away.

And Jesus answering saith unto them, Have faith in God.

Mark 11:22

You see, faith is calling those things that be not as though they were! I will say it again, Jesus is Faith!

(As it is written, I have made thee a father of many nations,) before him whom he believed, even God, who quickeneth the dead, and calleth those things which be not as though they were.

Romans 4:17

The doctor may have told you that there is no cure for that terminal cancer, there is no cure for the arthritis or for the blood pressure.

But I want you to know that God is able to heal you right know! Speak life and speak faith! Speak to that sickness to die and leave your body right now in the name of Jesus Christ. I do not care if you

44

are lying paralysed on a bed or sitting in a wheelchair. I command you right now to arise and walk in the name of Jesus Christ! Hallelujah! Amen.

For faith is calling forth those things that be not to come forth. We do not walk by what we see. We walk and operate by faith!

Have the doctors told you that you cannot have children? Receive your children now in the name of Jesus Christ! Are you struggling to get a job? Speak your job into existence! Tell yourself that you are the only one that will be offered the job at the interview. Are you struggling with immigration? Receive your indefinite stay right now in the name of Jesus Christ! The doctors, the employers and the lawyers may say that there is no hope for you but I am announcing to you right now, that Christ in us is the hope of glory! HALLELUJAH!

To whom God would make known what is the riches of the glory of this mystery among the Gentiles; which is Christ in you, the hope of glory:

Colossians 1:27

You Cannot Give a Good Offering without Faith

Everyone can give an offering but the offerings which please God are those given by faith. Giving an offering is a spiritual exercise and it must be accepted by God and not man. It is a Christian duty which is between the individual Christian and God. Your offering must stem from the faith that is in your heart.

You must never give grudgingly and unwillingly. You do not give because of anyone but you give to worship your God in a special way.

Every man according as he purposeth in his heart, so let him give; not grudgingly, or of necessity: FOR GOD LOVETH A CHEERFUL GIVER.

2 Corinthians 9:7

This word of God gives Cain and Abel as an example of two kinds of offering given by faith.

And Adam knew Eve his wife; and she conceived, and bare Cain, and said, I have gotten a man from the LORD.
And she again bare his brother Abel. And Abel was a keeper of sheep, but Cain was a tiller of the ground.

And in process of time it came to pass, that Cain brought of the fruit of the ground an offering unto the LORD. And Abel, he also brought of the firstlings of his flock and of the fat thereof.

And the LORD had respect unto Abel and to his offering: But unto Cain and to his offering he had not respect. And Cain was very wroth, and his countenance fell.

And the LORD said unto Cain, Why art thou wroth? and why is thy countenance fallen? If thou doest well, shalt thou not be accepted? and if thou doest not well, sin lieth at the door. And unto thee shall be his desire, and thou shalt rule over him.

Genesis 4:1-7

What was the difference between Abel's offering and his brother Cain's offering? Why did the Lord not accept Cain's offering? Now this is the secret, Abel's offering was offered with blood. The blood was a symbol of the blood of Jesus. And once, by faith, the offering is covered with the blood it is an excellent sacrifice.

By faith Abel offered unto God a more excellent sacrifice than Cain, by which he obtained witness that he was righteous, God testifying of his gifts: and by it he being dead yet speaketh.

Hebrews 11:4

The sheep Abel slaughtered was a symbol and signification of Jesus Christ as the Lamb of God.

The next day John seeth Jesus coming unto him, and saith, Behold the Lamb of God, which taketh away the sin of the world.

John 1:29

You Cannot Stand as a Christian without Faith

Not for that we have dominion over your faith, but are helpers of your joy: for BY FAITH YE STAND.

2 Corinthians 1:24

By faith we can stand the test of time and continue walking as Christians. In other words, our faith will enable us to abide in Christ. Often, people become Christians and after a few years, they fall by the wayside or drift away from the truth. But in order to be established in Christ, we must have faith that sustains us and strengthens us to overcome all obstacles. So then, your faith will cause you to stand trials, tribulations, persecutions and the attacks of men.

The word of God tells us that because of unbelief Christians have broken away. But you shall surely stand by faith!

Well; because of unbelief they were broken off, and THOU STANDEST BY FAITH. Be not highminded, but fear:
Romans 11:20

Faith is a shield. Many battles must be fought in the life of a Christian. As the enemy becomes enraged, there will be spiritual attacks on the believer. There are times you feel as if everything has collapsed on you and that you cannot endure any longer. But that is when we should use the shield of faith! With the shield of faith we can quench all the fiery darts of the wicked and still stand victorious.

Stand therefore, having your loins girt about with truth, and having on the breastplate of righteousness;

And your feet shod with the preparation of the gospel of peace;

Above all, taking the shield of faith, wherewith ye shall be able to quench all the fiery darts of the wicked.
Ephesians 6:14-16

And blessed is she that believed: for there shall be a performance of those things which were told her from the Lord.

Luke 1:45

Chapter 7

Jesus is Moved by Faith not Tears

Your faith will cause Jesus to rush to your rescue. He responds to your faith not to your tears. I have seen many people wallowing in their tears thinking that Jesus will have pity because of the amount they cry. But this is a lie. Wipe your tears from today and replace it with faith! For when you believe, there shall definitely be a performance. Jesus cannot help but answer your need when He sees faith in your heart and in your eyes.

And blessed is she that believed: for there shall be a performance of those things which were told her from the Lord.

Luke 1:45

I was once asked to pray for a lady who was constantly vomiting blood due to lung cancer. This lady could also not see properly and she was struggling to walk. In fact, she was using a Zimmer Frame to help her move around. Her condition had deteriorated so much that she could not even climb stairs. Her living room on the ground floor was now her bedroom. I visited this lady with four other people from my church, including her friend who had requested for us to go and pray for this lady.

As soon as we arrived at the house, I knew the lady was about to receive a notable miracle because her faith was glowing and she was ready to receive her healing. We started singing and praying and I asked for anointing oil. The word of God says in **James 5:14-15**, *"is there any sick among you? Let him call for the elders of the church and let them pray over him, anointing him with oil in the name of the Lord: And the prayer of faith shall save the sick and the Lord shall raise him up"*. So we began praying as directed by the word of God.

I laid my hand on her and suddenly the woman said "I can see". She then stood up and began to walk and said "I can walk". I took the Zimmer Frame and pushed it aside. Then I said, "today you shall see your bedroom which you have not seen for two years". I led her to the foot of the stairs and tried to guard her as she started climbing the stairs she had not used for two years. She turned to me and said, "Pastor, I am healed" and she climbed the flight of stairs to her bedroom faster than we could catch up! Glory to God! She danced all over her house just like the lame man at the beautiful gate when he was healed. We praised Almighty God with her and encouraged her to keep standing in faith. Glory be to Jesus who responds to the faith of His people!

About three weeks after we visited, I was preaching in church on a Sunday when we had a visitor! I saw this same lady open the doors and walk into the church without any mobility aid. She had come to give her testimony. She said "Pastor, after the prayers I went for a check-up at the doctors and to the glory of God, my doctor told me there is no more cancer in my lungs". Hallelujah! Blessed is she who has believed for there shall be a performance.

Jesus saw the faith in this lady and He responded to her need.

Another incredible testimony happened during our regular prayer and fasting programme called Break Every Chain. One evening, a lady came along who had been told about the powerful testimonies Almighty God was bringing forth. She was desperate to receive hers. She had twice carried a child in her womb and both times the child had died. The husband was unable to attend but she came full of faith.

During the service, the Spirit of the Lord led me to give her my jacket to wear. The instant she wore the jacket, her deliverance started to manifest. She was totally delivered from the demons that were tormenting her. I was again led by the Spirit of God to tell her to sleep with her husband that very night and that she would conceive again that night. The woman was full of faith and she believed. She followed the exact instructions of the Holy Spirit. I remember that I prayed for this lady on a Friday evening.

The following Wednesday, I received a call from the husband testifying that his wife was pregnant. Jesus again responded to the faith of this lady. As I am writing this book, they now have a beautiful baby girl just over a year old. All Glory and Praise be to Jesus!

The Bible has so many examples of Jesus responding to the faith of the people. Many of the people who received their healing were healed because of their faith. Below are several biblical examples of Jesus being moved because the faith of the people. Let your faith rise as you read these testimonies of faith.

The Woman with the Issue of Blood

And, behold, a woman, which was diseased with an issue of blood twelve years, came behind him, and touched the hem of his garment:

For she said within herself, If I may but touch his garment, I shall be whole.

But Jesus turned him about, and when he saw her, he said, Daughter, be of good comfort; THY FAITH HATH MADE THEE WHOLE. And the woman was made whole from that hour.

Matthew 9:20-22

The woman with the issue of blood suffered this shameful affliction for 12 years. She had spent her money and her time visiting different specialist doctors to no avail. She had looked for help from different sources but her situation did not change until she took a decision to try Jesus. Her faith so moved Jesus that she received her healing instantly. She touched Jesus' garments from behind without Him knowing and still the power of God flowed into the woman.

This woman's faith also reveals that even the clothes of an anointed man of God are anointed and that whatever a man of God touches is also anointed. When Jesus turned around, He could only say to her *"thy faith hath made thee whole"*.

The Two Blind Men

And when Jesus departed thence, two blind men followed him, crying, and saying, Thou Son of David, have mercy on us.

And when he was come into the house, the blind men came to him: and Jesus saith unto them, Believe ye that I am able to do this? They said unto him, Yea, Lord.

Then touched he their eyes, saying, ACCORDING TO YOUR FAITH BE IT UNTO YOU. And their eyes were opened; and Jesus straitly charged them, saying, See that no man know it.
Matthew 9:27-30

These two blind men followed Jesus expecting to receive their healing. They followed him relentlessly and cried to Him for their healing. I can imagine people saying to them "stop shouting and stop disturbing us" but these two could not be stopped. They were ready to receive their healing.

Their actions caused Jesus to pause and touch their eyes. Read the scripture carefully. Jesus asked them whether they had faith in Him and they responded with a resounding yes. And Jesus said to them *"according to your faith be it unto you"*. Healing and breakthroughs come as a result of your faith in Jesus and your readiness to receive.

The Ten Lepers

And as he entered into a certain village, there met him ten men that were lepers, which stood afar off: And they lifted up their voices, and said, Jesus, Master, have mercy on us.

And when he saw them, he said unto them, Go shew yourselves unto the priests. And it came to pass, that, as they went, they were cleansed.

And one of them, when he saw that he was healed, turned back, and with a loud voice glorified God, And fell down on his face at his feet, giving him thanks: and he was a Samaritan.

And Jesus answering said, Were there not ten cleansed? but where are the nine? There are not found that returned to give glory to God, save this stranger. And he said unto him, Arise, go thy way: THY FAITH HATH MADE THEE WHOLE.

Luke 17:12-19

In the Old Testament, lepers were considered unclean and they were outcast. This means these ten lepers were not supposed to be in that village as their uncleanness could contaminate anyone who came into contact with them. They were banished outside and were forbidden to come close to anyone. Read it for yourself.

And if there be in the bald head, or bald forehead, a white reddish sore; it is a leprosy sprung up in his bald head, or his bald forehead.

Then the priest shall look upon it: and, behold, if the rising of the sore be white reddish in his bald head, or in his bald forehead, as the leprosy appeareth in the skin of the flesh;

He is a leprous man, he is unclean: the priest shall pronounce him utterly unclean; his plague is in his head. And the leper in

whom the plague is, his clothes shall be rent, and his head bare, and he shall put a covering upon his upper lip, and shall cry, Unclean, unclean.

All the days wherein the plague shall be in him he shall be defiled; he is unclean: HE SHALL DWELL ALONE; WITHOUT THE CAMP SHALL HIS HABITATION BE.
Leviticus 13:42-46

In the previous scripture, in **Luke 17**, we see that the lepers stood afar off. They had to raise their voices and shout to be heard, saying *"Jesus, Master, have mercy on us"*. They were afraid to come close but nonetheless they decided that as long as the Master is here, we must receive our healing! They exhibited great faith and Jesus responded to their faith. Moreover, the one who went back to give God the glory was rewarded. Jesus said to him, *"thy faith hath made thee whole"*.

Blind Bartimaeus

And they came to Jericho: and as he went out of Jericho with his disciples and a great number of people, blind Bartimaeus, the son of Timaeus, sat by the highway side begging.

And when he heard that it was Jesus of Nazareth, he began to cry out, and say, Jesus, thou Son of David, have mercy on me. And many charged him that he should hold his peace: but he cried the more a great deal, Thou Son of David, have mercy on me.

And Jesus stood still, and commanded him to be called. And they call the blind man, saying unto him, Be of good comfort,

rise; he calleth thee. And he, casting away his garment, rose, and came to Jesus. And Jesus answered and said unto him, What wilt thou that I should do unto thee?

The blind man said unto him, Lord, that I might receive my sight. And Jesus said unto him, Go thy way; THY FAITH HATH MADE THEE WHOLE. And immediately he received his sight, and followed Jesus in the way.

Mark 10:46-52

This blind man's case is very similar to that of the ten lepers. When he heard that Jesus was in town, Bartimaeus knew that the moment had come for him to receive his sight. He had heard of many who had been healed when they came into contact with Jesus.

Like the lepers, he took action and began to cry out. The word of God says that many people told him to keep quiet but he refused to be silenced. Do not allow people to kill your faith by the things they say! Do not be concerned about people who tell you that you go to church too much or you pray too much! Keep your eyes fixed on Jesus and you shall receive your blessing. The blind man's actions made Jesus stand still and respond to his faith. Jesus heard the voice of faith and He could not help himself but to stop and heal Bartimaeus. Jesus said to him, *"thy faith hath made thee whole"*.

A Bed-bound Man with a Palsy

And it came to pass on a certain day, as he was teaching, that there were Pharisees and doctors of the law sitting by, which were come out of every town of Galilee, and Judaea, and

Jerusalem: and the power of the Lord was present to heal them.

And, behold, men brought in a bed a man which was taken with a palsy: and they sought means to bring him in, and to lay him before him.

And when they could not find by what way they might bring him in because of the multitude, they went upon the housetop, and let him down through the tiling with his couch into the midst before Jesus.

AND WHEN HE SAW THEIR FAITH, HE SAID UNTO HIM, MAN, THY SINS ARE FORGIVEN THEE.

Luke 5:17-20

The sick man's friends demonstrated great faith. They had to uncover someone's roof which was probably an illegal to do. They had only one thing in mind and they were not concerned about whatever got in their way. They were committed to getting their friend healed! Can you imagine sitting in church whilst the pastor is preaching and you see a sick person being lowered down from the roof of the building? Yet amazingly, this is what these friends did. Jesus responded to their faith; *"And when he saw their faith, he said unto him, Man, thy sins are forgiven thee"*.

I have prayed for a countless number of people and you can always tell those who have faith and those who do not. The faith people easily receive their breakthrough while the faithless struggle and battle with their problems all their lives.

You notice that in all the above scriptures that Jesus never said His anointing is healing the people. Jesus said, *"Thy faith has made thee whole"*. It is therefore not the anointing on the man of God alone that heals the people but it is the faith of the people connecting with the anointing on the man of God. This combination is what heals and causes deliverance to take place in the lives of the people. No matter how anointed a man of God is, if the people do not have faith, the Holy Spirit will not move.

Pastors, we must see where faith is and move towards faith. The lame man at the beautiful gate in **Acts 3** was looking at Peter and John expecting to receive something and he received his healing. Pray for the people who have faith and you will see results.

When an altar call is made to pray for people who need healing, some people stand there like statues expecting the pastor to work magic. They think it is the pastor who causes the healing to happen. No! This is wrong. The pastor is a vessel through which the anointing flows but your faith in God pulls that anointing out and causes healings to take place. In the examples above, everyone that Jesus healed was healed because of their faith and their action that accompanied their faith.

Faith is what move the mountains! It is faith that causes extraordinary miracles to happen and it is faith that will purchase you all the blessings of the kingdom of God. Faith is the currency in the kingdom of Almighty God.

That if thou shalt confess with thy mouth the Lord Jesus, and shalt believe in thine heart that God hath raised him from the dead, thou shalt be saved. For with the heart man believeth unto righteousness; and with the mouth confession is made unto salvation.

Romans 10:9-10

Chapter 8

Real Faith is of the Heart not in the Mind

Faith is not a mental exercise, it stems from the heart. Most people do not understand why the thing they are asking the Lord for has not come to pass. They do not realise that it is because they are only thinking it in their minds and it has not sunk into their hearts. Faith when it is borne of the heart produces results.

That if thou shalt confess with thy mouth the Lord Jesus, and shalt believe in thine heart that God hath raised him from the dead, thou shalt be saved.

For with the heart man believeth unto righteousness; and with the mouth confession is made unto salvation.

Romans 10:9-10

Look at this scripture carefully, the *heart* believes and the *mouth* confesses. When faith has so filled your heart, you cannot help it but to speak it with your mouth. The word of God says that if you will believe in your heart, you shall be saved.

Although faith is not in the mind, yet still, the thoughts of the mind can greatly affect your faith. Do not worry if your mind wavers but be very careful that doubt does not seep into your heart. If you allow doubts and uncertainties in the mind to enter your heart, it will generate fear in your heart. Fear will negate the faith that has built up in your heart and the results will be negative.

I have counselled people who worry so much that they enter into depression and fear. When you are depressed, you cannot focus and you cannot have faith. Therefore you must guard your mind from negative thoughts that can enter into your heart and negate your faith. Ensure that the thoughts that flow through your mind are positive thoughts that will have positive effects on the faith you have in your heart. The Bible encourages us to hold our faith in a good conscience in order that we do not ruin our faith. Read it for yourself.

Holding faith, and a good conscience; which some having put away concerning faith have made shipwreck:

1 Timothy 1:19

Be careful not to allow the activities of the mind to cause unbelief to be formed in your heart. Faith comes from the heart and unbelief also stems from the heart.

Take heed, brethren, lest there be in any of you an evil heart of unbelief, in departing from the living God.

Hebrews 3:12

So then faith cometh by hearing, and hearing by the word of God.

Romans 10:17

Chapter 9

How to Receive Faith

There are three ways that a person can receive faith into the heart. The starting point is to be born again or receive Jesus Christ as your Lord and Saviour. The journey of faith begins when you believe and confess that Jesus Christ is Lord.

That if thou shalt confess with thy mouth the Lord Jesus, and shalt believe in thine heart that God hath raised him from the dead, thou shalt be saved.

For with the heart man believeth unto righteousness; and with the mouth confession is made unto salvation.

Romans 10:9-10

Secondly, after being born again, you must build your faith with the word of God because faith comes by hearing and hearing by the word of God. The more of the word of God that is in you, the more faith you will have. My book on **Three Dimensions of Man** explains further about the practical steps to having a solid foundation of the word of God. The Holy Scriptures will help you to build up your faith in the Lord.

So then faith cometh by hearing, and hearing by the word of God.
Romans 10:17

Thirdly, you must pray daily and fellowship daily with the Lord to increase your faith. Jesus Himself is faith so the more you fellowship with Him, the more faith you receive. You can pray to the Lord and ask Him to increase your faith just as the disciples prayed. You can also pray in the Holy Ghost to build up your faith.

And the apostles said unto the Lord, Increase our faith.
Luke 17:5

But ye, beloved, building up yourselves on your most holy faith, praying in the Holy Ghost,
Jude 1:20

For I say, through the grace given unto me, to every man that is among you, not to think of himself more highly than he ought to think; but to think soberly, according as God hath dealt to every man the measure of faith.

Romans 12:3

Chapter 10

Types of Faith

There are different types of faith mentioned in the Bible. These types of faith are all given by the Holy Spirit to the believer. These are the **Measure of Faith** given at salvation, the **Gift of Faith** imparted as the Holy Spirit wills and the **Fruit of Faith** which is a fruit of the Spirit exhibited by matured Christians. Let us now look at each of these in turn.

Measure of Faith

Firstly, faith is given at salvation. This initial faith that is given at salvation can be measured. Each Christian is given a certain measure or a portion. The Christian must then begin his or her Christian walk by building upon this faith to increase it.

For I say, through the grace given unto me, to every man that is among you, not to think of himself more highly than he ought to think; but to think soberly, according as God hath dealt to every man THE MEASURE OF FAITH.

Romans 12:3

Having then gifts differing according to the grace that is given to us, whether prophecy, let us prophesy according to the PROPORTION OF FAITH;

Romans 12:6

Every born again Christian has a measure of faith. This faith is what enables you to be saved upon hearing the glorious gospel of Jesus Christ. The faith to believe in the Lord is given at salvation.

But as many as received him, to them gave he power to become the sons of God, even to them that believe on his name:

John 1:12

There is also mustard seed faith and there is little faith. These are all measures of faith.

And the Lord said, If ye had faith as a GRAIN OF MUSTARD SEED, ye might say unto this sycamine tree, Be thou plucked up by the root, and be thou planted in the sea; and it should obey you.

Luke 17:6

Wherefore, if God so clothe the grass of the field, which to day is, and to morrow is cast into the oven, shall he not much more clothe you, O ye of LITTLE FAITH?

Matthew 6:30

And he saith unto them, Why are ye fearful, O ye of LITTLE FAITH? Then he arose, and rebuked the winds and the sea; and there was a great calm.

Matthew 8:26

And immediately Jesus stretched forth his hand, and caught him, and said unto him, O thou of LITTLE FAITH, wherefore didst thou doubt?

Matthew 14:31

This little faith must increase by building upon it. The apostles prayed and said *"Lord increase our faith"* in **Luke 17:5**. Faith can therefore be increased. You can have more of Jesus in you or can have less of Him. The faith that was given to you at salvation must not remain the same, it must grow.

The majority of Christians fall by the wayside when they experience trials and tribulations. But those that have built up their faith in the Lord shall overcome every obstacle that comes their way. We must be rooted firm in Christ Jesus.

Rooted and built up in him, and stablished in the faith, as ye have been taught, abounding therein with thanksgiving.

Colossians 2:7

We are also cautioned by the scriptures to operate according to the portion of faith we have in Jesus. If you have never prayed for the sick to be healed, you will not have the faith to pray for someone to rise from a wheelchair.

For as we have many members in one body, and all members have not the same office: So we, being many, are one body in Christ, and every one members one of another.

Having then gifts differing according to the grace that is given to us, whether prophecy, let us prophesy ACCORDING TO THE PROPORTION OF FAITH; Or ministry, let us wait on our ministering: or he that teacheth, on teaching;

Or he that exhorteth, on exhortation: he that giveth, let him do it with simplicity; he that ruleth, with diligence; he that sheweth mercy, with cheerfulness.

Romans 12:4-8

It is so important for our faith to mature in the Lord. If we do not, we will suffer in this world because the only thing that overcomes the world is our faith in Christ Jesus.

For whatsoever is born of God overcometh the world: and this is the victory that overcometh the world, even our faith.

1 John 5:4

I have come to understand that the more of the word you have in you the more your faith increases and is built up.

So then faith cometh by hearing, and hearing by the word of God.

Romans 10:17

We must therefore earnestly desire and use all means available to get the word of God to feed our spirit. Apart from reading the Bible, you can also invest in anointed Christian books and preaching audio and video messages. Christians should listen to more anointed Christian worship songs. This is good and certainly better than listening to worldly songs that will bring demons into your life. But first and foremost, you have to understand that it is the WORD that brings faith, it is the WORD that builds us up and it is the WORD that transforms us from glory to glory.

Gift of Faith

The scripture passage below talks of the spiritual gifts given by the Holy Spirit. Let us examine it closely, especially verse nine, where the word of God talks about faith given by the Holy Spirit.

Now concerning spiritual gifts, brethren, I would not have you ignorant.

Ye know that ye were Gentiles, carried away unto these dumb idols, even as ye were led.

Wherefore I give you to understand, that no man speaking by the Spirit of God calleth Jesus accursed: and that no man can say that Jesus is the Lord, but by the Holy Ghost.

Now there are diversities of gifts, but the same Spirit.

And there are differences of administrations, but the same Lord.

And there are diversities of operations, but it is the same God which worketh all in all.

But the manifestation of the Spirit is given to every man to profit withal.

For to one is given by the Spirit the word of wisdom; to another the word of knowledge by the same Spirit;

TO ANOTHER FAITH by the same Spirit; to another the gifts of healing by the same Spirit;

To another the working of miracles; to another prophecy; to another discerning of spirits; to another divers kinds of tongues; to another the interpretation of tongues:

1 Corinthians 12: 1-10

In **1 Corinthians 12:9**, the word of God talks about the gift of faith given by the Holy Spirit. We must realise that there is a difference between the gift of faith imparted by the Holy Spirit and the measure of faith which is given at the time of salvation.

As with the other gifts of the Holy Spirit, such as working of miracles and healings, you cannot force yourself to manifest them anytime you want them to operate. A pastor or a prophet is not the worker of miracles. Jesus is the worker of miracles and He manifests these gifts through vessels that avail themselves to be used by the Lord. Therefore, the gift of faith is released or imparted by the Holy Ghost to a believer as and when needed.

I have been in services where the anointing comes upon me as a cloak and at that moment, the gift of faith is released. It is lifted off once the service is over. There is nothing impossible for the gift of faith. To men it is impossible but to God, all things are possible. This is the GIFT OF FAITH or what people call "the God kind of faith".

It is the gift of faith that causes peculiar miracles beyond our imaginations to happen. It is the gift of faith that raises the dead, causes the cripple to walk and empties the wheelchairs. It is the gift of faith that causes the deaf ears to open and the dumb to speak. It is the gift of faith the causes demons to be cast out.

Apostles Peter and John went to the temple to pray one day. As they went, a certain man was sitting at the gate begging. The word of God tells us in **Acts 3** that this man was lame from birth. He was now 38 years old with this same infirmity but it took the operation of the gift of faith to set this man up on his feet for the first time in his life. The will of God for this man was not to beg for money. God had a better plan for him and it took the gift of faith that operated through Apostle Peter to free him from this condition. Read it for yourself.

Now Peter and John went up together into the temple at the hour of prayer, being the ninth hour. And a certain man lame from his mother's womb was carried, whom they laid daily at the gate of the temple which is called Beautiful, to ask alms of them that entered into the temple;

Who seeing Peter and John about to go into the temple asked an alms. And Peter, fastening his eyes upon him with John, said, Look on us. And he gave heed unto them, expecting to receive something of them.

Then Peter said, Silver and gold have I none; but such as I have give I thee: In the name of Jesus Christ of Nazareth rise up and walk. And he took him by the right hand, and lifted him up: and immediately his feet and ankle bones received strength.

And he leaping up stood, and walked, and entered with them into the temple, walking, and leaping, and praising God.

Acts 3:1-8

Instant Miracles through the Gift of Faith

The gift of faith imparted by the Holy Spirit produces instant miracles. It operated throughout the life and ministry of Jesus. In the scripture below you see the gift of faith manifesting. The woman who was infirm for 18 years was able to lift herself up immediately. She received her healing and miracle instantly!

And, behold, there was a woman which had a spirit of infirmity eighteen years, and was bowed together, and could in no wise lift up herself.

And when Jesus saw her, he called her to him, and said unto her, Woman, thou art loosed from thine infirmity.

And he laid his hands on her: and IMMEDIATELY she was made straight, and glorified God.

Luke 13:11

There are several instances in the word of God where the gift of faith manifested in the life of Jesus.

And it came to pass, that as he was come nigh unto Jericho, a certain blind man sat by the way side begging: And hearing the multitude pass by, he asked what it meant. And they told him, that Jesus of Nazareth passeth by.

And he cried, saying, Jesus, thou Son of David, have mercy on me. And they which went before rebuked him, that he should hold his peace: but he cried so much the more, Thou Son of David, have mercy on me.

And Jesus stood, and commanded him to be brought unto him: and when he was come near, he asked him, Saying, What wilt thou that I shall do unto thee? And he said, Lord, that I may receive my sight.

And Jesus said unto him, Receive thy sight: thy faith hath saved thee. And IMMEDIATELY he received his sight, and followed him, glorifying God: and all the people, when they saw it, gave praise unto God.

Luke 18:35-43

When he was come down from the mountain, great multitudes followed him.

And, behold, there came a leper and worshipped him, saying, Lord, if thou wilt, thou canst make me clean.

And Jesus put forth his hand, and touched him, saying, I will; be thou clean. And IMMEDIATELY his leprosy was cleansed.

Matthew 8:1-3

And as they departed from Jericho, a great multitude followed him. And, behold, two blind men sitting by the way side, when they heard that Jesus passed by, cried out, saying, Have mercy on us, O Lord, thou Son of David.

And the multitude rebuked them, because they should hold their peace: but they cried the more, saying, Have mercy on us, O Lord, thou Son of David.

And Jesus stood still, and called them, and said, What will ye that I shall do unto you? They say unto him, Lord, that our eyes may be opened.

So Jesus had compassion on them, and touched their eyes: and **IMMEDIATELY** their eyes received sight, and they followed him.
Matthew 20:29-34

But Simon's wife's mother lay sick of a fever, and anon they tell him of her.

And he came and took her by the hand, and lifted her up; and **IMMEDIATELY** the fever left her, and she ministered unto them.
Mark 1:30-31

And again he entered into Capernaum after some days; and it was noised that he was in the house. And straightway many were gathered together, insomuch that there was no room to receive them, no, not so much as about the door: and he preached the word unto them.

And they come unto him, bringing one sick of the palsy, which was borne of four. And when they could not come nigh unto him for the press, they uncovered the roof where he was: and when they had broken it up, they let down the bed wherein the sick of the palsy lay.

When Jesus saw their faith, he said unto the sick of the palsy, Son, thy sins be forgiven thee. But there were certain of the scribes sitting there, and reasoning in their hearts, Why doth this man thus speak blasphemies? who can forgive sins but God only?

And immediately when Jesus perceived in his spirit that they so reasoned within themselves, he said unto them, Why reason ye these things in your hearts? Whether is it easier to say to the sick of the palsy, Thy sins be forgiven thee; or to say, Arise, and take up thy bed, and walk?

But that ye may know that the Son of man hath power on earth to forgive sins, (he saith to the sick of the palsy,) I say unto thee, Arise, and take up thy bed, and go thy way into thine house.

And IMMEDIATELY he arose, took up the bed, and went forth before them all; insomuch that they were all amazed, and glorified God, saying, We never saw it on this fashion.

Mark 2:1-12

Fruit of Faith

The fruit of faith is different from the measure of faith and the gift of faith in that the fruit of faith is formed in a believer as they mature and encounter troubles, tribulations and persecutions.

But the fruit of the Spirit is love, joy, peace, longsuffering, gentleness, goodness, FAITH, Meekness, temperance: against such there is no law.

Galatians 5:22-23

A believer who has the fruit of faith formed in them will not waver when troubles arise in life because they knows that God is God and God can overcome any situation. It is this type of faith that enables Christians to overcome the world.

For whatsoever is born of God OVERCOMETH the world: and this is the victory that overcometh the world, even our FAITH.

1 John 5:4

The fruit of a tree is produced when the tree is matured to the point where it can bear fruit. The fruit is the edible part of the tree. In other words, the fruit of faith is the matured character shown by a believer when trials occur and the believer does not abandon God. Many Christians give up their Christian life when things are not going well for them. You see, the fruit of faith forms patience in a believer. A believer with the fruit of faith has patience to wait for their time, knowing that in God's time, He will make everything beautiful.

He hath made every thing beautiful in his time: also he hath set the world in their heart, so that no man can find out the work that God maketh from the beginning to the end.

Ecclesiastes 3:11

Through the fruit of faith and patience, a believer will inherit and receive every promise concerning their life. Do not give up! Have faith and believe that your God is able to do more than you ask or even think.

That ye be not slothful, but followers of them who through FAITH and PATIENCE inherit the promises.

Hebrews 6:12

The fruit of faith in a nutshell is faith that has been tested and tried. That is what causes it to mature and form a refined and unquestionable character in the believer. A believer who is unmovable, unshakable and steadfast and who lives by faith and not by sight has the fruit of faith.

My brethren, count it all joy when ye fall into divers temptations;

Knowing this, that the trying of your FAITH WORKETH PATIENCE.

But let patience have her perfect work, that ye may be perfect and entire, wanting nothing.

James 1:2-4

And not only so, but we glory in tribulations also: knowing that tribulation worketh patience; And patience, experience; and experience, hope:

Romans 5:3-4

And we know that all things work together for good to them that love God, to them who are the called according to his purpose.

Romans 8:28

For our light affliction, which is but for a moment, worketh for us a far more exceeding and eternal weight of glory;

2 Corinthians 4:17

SECTION III

❧

Activating and Building your Faith

Through faith we understand that the worlds were framed by the word of God, so that things which are seen were not made of things which do appear.

Hebrews 11:3

Chapter 11

The Power of Faith

T here is tremendous power when faith is put into action. The power of God is always available to believers but that which unlocks the power is faith. A believer is able to tap into this power to his or her benefit through faith. Here are just three areas through which the power of faith can be demonstrated: **The Power of Restoration, the Power to Release the Unknown and the Power to Move Mountains.**

The Power of Restoration

In **Genesis 1:1-2**, the word of God says that the earth was without form and void and darkness was upon the face of the deep.

In the beginning God created the heaven and the earth.

And the earth was without form, and void; and darkness was upon the face of the deep. And the Spirit of God moved upon the face of the waters.

Genesis 1:1- 2

This means that the world was in total chaos and it required restoration. The Lord used the power of faith to repair and to restore the world. Can you imagine the power that was needed by Almighty God to restore this earth back to its former state? The power to recreate the earth, the trees, animals and the power to arrange everything on the earth in perfect order again. It is certainly more power than all the power generators on this planet! The good news is that this power was embedded in the power of faith!

> **Through faith we understand that the worlds were framed by the word of God, so that things which are seen were not made of things which do appear.**
>
> **Hebrews 11:3**

The above passage of scripture makes it clear that the worlds were framed by the word of God. This could not happen without faith. When the Lord opened His mouth and spoke through faith; the heavens, the earth and under the earth were instantly perfectly restored.

The word "Framed" in the above verse means *to repair* and *to restore*. Restoration of life is in the power of faith. The word of God tells us that without Jesus, that is, without faith, was not anything made that was made. Jesus is faith and without Jesus, the Lord could not have restored the world.

> **All things were made by him; and without him was not any thing made that was made.**
>
> **John 1:3**

> **For by him were all things created, that are in heaven, and that are in earth, visible and invisible, whether they be thrones, or dominions, or principalities, or powers: all things were created by him, and for him:**
>
> **Colossians 1:16**

If you have given up on life, try Jesus and the power in His name. *At the mention of His name, anything that has deteriorated in your life shall be restored! Every sickness shall be removed! Your entire life will receive meaning and be perfected by the power in the name of Jesus!*

The power of creation is in the power of faith. From today, speak to create the good things you expect to see in your life. Without Jesus was not anything made that was made. The word of God specifically says that by Him were all things created. The faith that repaired and restored the world was Jesus. *I see you being restored by the power in the name of Jesus!*

The Power to Release the Unknown

Abraham was a man of faith. The Lord had promised him that he would be a father of many nations. Yet the time he received the promise there was no sign of him ever having a child. Both Abraham and his wife Sarah were very old and could no longer naturally conceive. But the word of God says that Abraham believed the Lord God who calls the things which we cannot see into existence.

The truth is that everything you need in this life already exists in the supernatural realm. The currency to buy those things is the currency of faith. Faith has the power to release the unknown. *You can call forth your children now! You can call forth your job and you can call forth your future into being by the power of faith!* The Lord called forth Abraham's future by the power of faith and today, we are all the children of Abraham.

(As it is written, I have made thee a father of many nations,) before him whom he believed, even God, who quickeneth the dead, and calleth those things which be not as though they were.

Romans 4:17

Ho, every one that thirsteth, come ye to the waters, and he that hath no money; come ye, buy, and eat; yea, come, buy wine and milk without money and without price.

Isaiah 55:1

The above scripture from **Isaiah 55** is the demonstration of the power of faith. The Lord is commanding you to unlock your needs in the spiritual realm, not with money but with faith. When you open your mouth, speak faith out of your heart. Your blessings in the spiritual realm shall surely be released to you physically.

Are you hungry and thirsty for a blessing? Are you desperate? Speak the word of faith that is your mouth right now and it shall be released to you in Jesus name!

I once visited a couple and as I was leaving, I asked the wife what she wanted the Lord to do for her. As soon as I asked, the wife burst into tears so I asked what the matter was. She began to narrate her ordeal. This couple had only recently married and they could not freely enjoy their marriage union. The lady explained that she has developed a cist on her back side that was so painful she could not even sit down for long periods. She had already had one operation to remove it but another cist had started developing again. She was now due for another operation within the next few weeks.

I told her that she will not need to do the operation and I asked her if she believed that the Lord was able to heal her in that same instant. Thanks be to God that she had faith to receive the unknown! I prayed with them and even prophesied that she was going to conceive soon. The husband said that he was not yet ready for a child but I still had to say what the Lord was telling me to say. I then left.

According to the lady, in the night she had a dream where she saw that the cist had burst. When she woke up, the cist had truly burst! As I am writing this book, to the glory of the Lord Jesus, the lady is totally healed from the cist, she did not undergo any surgery and the couple have been blessed with a beautiful child. Jesus, who is faith Himself, is able to bring into your life the unknown blessings that belong to you.

Jesus was standing at the tomb of Lazarus who had died for four days and the body was foul-smelling. The Pharisees were standing there watching whether this man who calls himself Jesus was able to call forth Lazarus who has been buried for so long. But Jesus stood before the tomb and lifted His hands into the heavens and prayed. After He had prayed, He said *"Lazarus, come forth"* and Lazarus was instantly revived. His spirit came back into his body. Thanks be to Jesus!

Jesus saith unto her, Said I not unto thee, that, if thou wouldest believe, thou shouldest see the glory of God? Then they took away the stone from the place where the dead was laid.

And Jesus lifted up his eyes, and said, Father, I thank thee that thou hast heard me. And I knew that thou hearest me always: but because of the people which stand by I said it, that they may believe that thou hast sent me.

And when he thus had spoken, he cried with a loud voice, Lazarus, come forth.

And he that was dead came forth, bound hand and foot with graveclothes: and his face was bound about with a napkin. Jesus saith unto them, Loose him, and let him go.

John 11:40-44

From today, do not be sad about the things you do not have. Just call them into being by faith!

The Power to Move Mountains

The mountain is an impossible situation. It is a difficulty that cannot be dealt with easily, it is a problem and it is an unfortunate circumstance. Nevertheless, every seemingly impossible situation has a solution. For that which is impossible with men is possible to the Lord! The power of faith is able to remove all impossibilities out of your life. The crooked places in your life can be straightened by the power of faith. By faith, whatsoever is possible to God is also possible to a born again Christian.

One day, a man brought his sick child to the disciples to cure him. But the disciples were unable to do so because they lacked faith. When Jesus came on the scene, He cast out the devil from the child and the child was instantly freed from that evil sickness. But look at what Jesus told the disciples.

And Jesus said unto them, Because of your unbelief: for verily I say unto you, If ye have faith as a grain of mustard seed, ye shall say unto this mountain, Remove hence to yonder place; and it shall remove; and NOTHING SHALL BE IMPOSSIBLE UNTO YOU.
Matthew 17:20

He plainly said that if they had faith, nothing shall be impossible to them. This is amazing and it gives Christians the understanding of the power of faith.

There was a lady in the church who had fibroids at the mouth of her womb and was constantly bleeding and in pain. Because of the position of the fibroids, her doctors had decided on surgery and that her womb would also be removed. During our Break Every Chain programme, the Spirit of God led me to call this lady forward and pray for her. After the programme, she went for a check-up and the fibroids had disappeared from her womb. As I am writing this book, this lady still has her womb and is fibroid free. To God be all the Glory!

There are many things that seem impossible in this life. One of these things is the ability to raise the dead. It is virtually impossible to bring a dead person back to life but I am announcing to you that the power of faith is able to raise the dead back to life. For with faith nothing shall be impossible.

In **Hebrews 11:35**, the word of God tells us that by faith, women receive their dead back to life again. I once watched a video testimony by Evangelist Reinhard Bonke. It contained a clip of a woman's testimony of how her husband had died and she refused for the husband to be buried because of this very scripture below;

Women received their dead raised to life again: and others were tortured, not accepting deliverance; that they might obtain a better resurrection:

Hebrews 11:35

Relatives tried to quench her faith but the woman persisted in standing by faith on this scripture. She even told the same relatives that the Evangelist Reinhard Bonke was having a crusade in town and that she would take her husband there and the husband will come back to life. She took the body of the husband in an ambulance and they drove to the crusade ground. The body of the husband was placed under the crusade ground where the Evangelist was preaching. While the preaching was going on, the spirit of God revived the dead husband back to life! Hallelujah!

This woman had faith and because she had faith, the impossible was possible to her. *I see all that things which are impossible in your life being made possible in the name of Jesus!*

Faith knows no limit and nothing can stand in the way of a person who is full of faith. There is a fascinating passage of scripture in **Mark 11**. I really love this scripture passage because it shows me the unstoppable power of faith.

Jesus was hungry and He went to the fig tree that He might get some fruits to eat. But there was no fruit on the tree. The amazing thing is that the word of God says it was not yet time for the fig tree to bear fruit. And yet still, Jesus commanded the fig tree to wither by the power of faith and it completely withered. The disciples were amazed that even trees could respond to the power of faith.

And on the morrow, when they were come from Bethany, he was hungry: And seeing a fig tree afar off having leaves, he came, if haply he might find any thing thereon: and when he came to it, he found nothing but leaves; for the time of figs was not yet.

And Jesus answered and said unto it, No man eat fruit of thee hereafter for ever. And his disciples heard it.

And they come to Jerusalem: and Jesus went into the temple, and began to cast out them that sold and bought in the temple, and overthrew the tables of the moneychangers, and the seats of them that sold doves; And would not suffer that any man should carry any vessel through the temple. And he taught, saying unto them, Is it not written, My house shall be called of all nations the house of prayer? but ye have made it a den of thieves. And the scribes and chief priests heard it, and sought how they might destroy him: for they feared him, because all the people was astonished at his doctrine.

And when even was come, he went out of the city. And in the morning, as they passed by, they saw the fig tree dried up from the roots. And Peter calling to remembrance saith unto him, Master, behold, the fig tree which thou cursedst is withered away.

And Jesus answering saith unto them, HAVE FAITH IN GOD. For verily I say unto you, That whosoever shall say unto this mountain, Be thou removed, and be thou cast into the sea; and shall not doubt in his heart, but shall believe that those things which he saith shall come to pass; he shall have whatsoever he saith.

Mark 11:12

Anything that has been created by the living God responds to faith. Such is the power that is encapsulated in faith. Jesus told the disciples to have faith in God and every mountain in their path shall be removed. *Receive the faith that makes impossible things possible in the name of Jesus!*

And Jesus answering saith unto them, Have faith in God.

For verily I say unto you, That whosoever shall say unto this mountain, Be thou removed, and be thou cast into the sea; and shall not doubt in his heart, but shall believe that those things which he saith shall come to pass; he shall have whatsoever he saith.

Therefore I say unto you, What things soever ye desire, when ye pray, believe that ye receive them, and ye shall have them.

Mark 11:22-24

Chapter 12

Activating the Power of Faith

I have noticed that in this world, those who do not speak are always taken advantage of. When you are too quiet in life, a lot of good things will pass you by. Those who speak are always in a position to receive something. **Matthew 7:7** says *"ask and you shall receive, seek and you shall find, knock and it shall be opened unto you"*. In **John 16:24**, the Lord said, *"Hitherto have ye asked nothing in my name, ask and ye shall receive that your joy may be full"*. So even with our Creator, those who keep quiet and never ask, receive nothing. If you speak life, you will reap life and if you speak death, you reap death.

Speaking

And Jesus answering saith unto them, Have faith in God.

For verily I say unto you, That whosoever shall say unto this mountain, Be thou removed, and be thou cast into the sea; and shall not doubt in his heart, but shall believe that those things which he saith shall come to pass; he shall have whatsoever he saith.

Therefore I say unto you, What things soever ye desire, when ye pray, believe that ye receive them, and ye shall have them.

Mark 11:22-24

Death and life are in the power of the tongue: and they that love it shall eat the fruit thereof.

Proverbs 18:21

Speaking therefore activates faith to deal with any obstacle. Speak to the situations in your life. Speak to that evil disease and it will give way. Speak to the mountains in your life. Say unto that mountain, "be thou be removed and cast into the sea" and it shall be done by faith.

The woman with the issue of blood in **Matthew 9:21** said to herself, *"if I may but touch His garment, I will be made perfectly whole"*. And as soon as she touched the hem of Jesus' garment, she was truly made perfectly whole. In the Old Testament, in **Leviticus 15:25-31**, women who bled for more than their menstrual cycle were regarded as unclean. They were separated from the general public until they were pronounced clean by the priest.

This woman should not have been in the public place where Jesus was and by law, she was forbidden from touching people. That is why Jesus said to her, *"daughter, be of good comfort, thy faith has made thee whole"*. The woman was afraid of being questioned as to why she touched Jesus. But she spoke by faith within herself. Speaking gives you boldness to act on the word of God. **I always say to myself and to my church that whatever Satan has said I will not have, I have and I possess.** *And I say to you right now, that whatever Satan has hindered you from having or receiving, you have it now in Jesus name!*

Mark 10:46-52 tells us that Bartimaeus was both blind and a beggar. But one day, he came to the realisation that blindness and begging was not his portion and it was certainly not the will of God for his life. As he sat at the gate begging, he heard a great multitude chanting the name of Jesus and he knew that the master was passing by. The word of God states that when he heard that it was Jesus, he began to *"cry out and say"*. People tried to shut him up, but the word of God says that he began to cry out and speak even louder until Jesus stood still and commanded him to come. The blind man received his sight because he learnt how to cry out and speak.

Only Believe

And Jesus said unto the centurion, Go thy way; and as thou hast believed, so be it done unto thee. And his servant was healed in the selfsame hour.

Matthew 8:13

Jesus said unto him, If thou canst believe, all things are possible to him that believeth.

Mark 9:23

The key to results is the key of believing. *As thou have believed so be it done unto you.* When the Master sees your faith, He has no option than to act. Believe in the word of God and act on the word. The centurion said, *"Master just speak the word and my servant will be healed"*, and the servant was healed in that same hour.

You see, all things that are possible to God are also possible to all those who believe in Him. *"For with God all things are possible"*

(Matthew 19:26). Therefore believing is actually the master key to your breakthroughs, your healing and your blessing. ***Is there anything in your life that seems impossible? Well, now you have the solution. Only believe!***

The phrase "your faith" is common to all the people who were healed by Jesus. Jesus uses phrases such as; *"thy faith has made thee whole" (Mark 10:52), (Matthew 9:22), "According to your faith be it unto you" (Matthew 9:29-30).*

So we also learn that without "your faith", Jesus does nothing. He is only moved by your faith. The word of God shows us in **Luke 5:20** that Jesus sees your faith. The Master can see your faith and when He sees your faith, He moves on your behalf. The man with the palsy received his healing because his friends had faith that Jesus was able to heal him and they found every means possible for Jesus to see him.

And, behold, men brought in a bed a man which was taken with a palsy: and they sought means to bring him in, and to lay him before him.

And when they could not find by what way they might bring him in because of the multitude, they went upon the housetop, and let him down through the tiling with his couch into the midst before Jesus.

And when he saw their faith, he said unto him, Man, thy sins are forgiven thee. And the scribes and the Pharisees began to reason, saying, Who is this which speaketh blasphemies? Who can forgive sins, but God alone?

But when Jesus perceived their thoughts, he answering said unto them, What reason ye in your hearts? Whether is easier, to say, Thy sins be forgiven thee; or to say, Rise up and walk? But that ye may know that the Son of man hath power upon earth to forgive sins, (he said unto the sick of the palsy,) I say unto thee, Arise, and take up thy couch, and go into thine house.

And immediately he rose up before them, and took up that whereon he lay, and departed to his own house, glorifying God. And they were all amazed, and they glorified God, and were filled with fear, saying, We have seen strange things to day.

Luke 5:18-26

Action

Faith demands action and without action, faith does not move. I was ministering in church one Sunday and the Spirit of the Lord led me to pray for a lady and tell her to pray and fast for three days for her family. After the service, the lady came and opened up to me that she was having immigration problems. Before that, I did not know about this immigration issue.

She explained to me that she had left her child behind in her home country. She was now trying to bring the child to join her but it was proving difficult. Her child had been asked to do a DNA test and the test had come back negative. The lady said "How could this be for my own child?" But still she did not give up. She asked me to remember them in prayers. So we believed God for a breakthrough.

But I tell you the truth, this woman is a woman of faith. She acted upon the word and she believed that there shall be a performance. After praying and fasting, her faith was strengthened. She believed so much that on the day of the second DNA test she was on the phone with her child saying "God is able to do it". This time, the second DNA test proved that the child was truly hers. Glory be to God! She acted upon the word and she received her answer.

Faith demands an action in order for it to be activated. For faith without works is dead!

Even so faith, if it hath not works, is dead, being alone
James 2:17

After you have prayed that God should give you a job, you have to prepare your CV and apply for jobs. You have to attend interviews so that God can give you a job. If you sit at one place and pray that God give me a job without CV and interviews, you may never get a job. The word "Works" in **James 2:17** means *doings*. It implies that faith without *doings, activities* or *action* is a dead faith. ***I see you receiving your blessings as you act upon the word of God in Jesus name!***

And the Lord said, If ye had faith as a grain of mustard seed, ye might say unto this sycamine tree, Be thou plucked up by the root, and be thou planted in the sea; and it should obey you.

Luke 17:6

Chapter 13

Various Kinds of Faith

There are various kinds of faith that the word of God describes in the Bible. In the previous chapters, we looked at the *types of faith* which were: the measure of faith, the gift of faith and the fruit of faith. However, the various kinds of faith are not like these. The various kinds of faith are exhibited by believers under certain situations and circumstances. It is vital that you know the kind of faith to operate under when faced with a particular situation. You can either overcome by the faith you are using or be defeated because of your faith. Jesus often told the disciples the kind of faith they were operating under during certain situations they faced.

Mustard Seed Faith

And the Lord said, IF YE HAD FAITH AS A GRAIN OF MUSTARD SEED, ye might say unto this sycamine tree,

Be thou plucked up by the root, and be thou planted in the sea; and it should obey you.

Luke 17:6

Before salvation, the Holy Spirit imparts faith to the unbeliever to enable them to be saved. As the word is being preached, it also births faith in the unbelievers' heart. In that instant, that faith enables the unbeliever to accept Jesus Christ as their Lord and Saviour. The word of God says in **John 1:12** that to those that believed on Him, He gave them the power to become the sons of God.

Mustard seed faith is so powerful that it causes eternal salvation to occur. That is why Jesus said that if you have faith as a mustard seed, you can speak to the sycamore tree or the mountain to be removed and it shall be done. After you are saved, your faith is still a mustard seed faith. It is very powerful but it must not remain a mustard seed, it must grow.

Weak Faith

And being NOT WEAK IN FAITH, he considered not his own body now dead, when he was about an hundred years old, neither yet the deadness of Sara's womb:

He staggered not at the promise of God through unbelief; but was strong in faith, giving glory to God;

Romans 4:19-20

Him that is WEAK IN THE FAITH receive ye, but not to doubtful disputations. For one believeth that he may eat all things: another, who is weak, eateth herbs.

Let not him that eateth despise him that eateth not; and let not him which eateth not judge him that eateth: for God hath received him.

Romans 14:1-3

A person who has a weak faith is shaken by the circumstances of life. When the circumstances get tough, such a person loses faith. A person with a weak faith therefore walks by sight. Once the condition looks good, they have faith and when the condition worsens, faith is lost. Faith knows no limit for whatever seems impossible to men, with God, it is possible. The word of God says that Abraham did not consider the deadness of his body or the deadness of Sarah's womb but he believed that God was able to perform. The weak kind of faith can be developed and strengthened with the word of God.

Little Faith

Wherefore, if God so clothe the grass of the field, which to day is, and to morrow is cast into the oven, shall he not much more clothe you, O YE OF LITTLE FAITH?

Matthew 6:30

And he saith unto them, Why are ye fearful, O YE OF LITTLE FAITH? Then he arose, and rebuked the winds and the sea; and there was a great calm.

Matthew 8:26

And immediately Jesus stretched forth his hand, and caught him, and said unto him, O THOU OF LITTLE FAITH, wherefore didst thou doubt?

Matthew 14:31

Which when Jesus perceived, he said unto them, O YE OF LITTLE FAITH, why reason ye among yourselves, because ye have brought no bread?

Matthew 16:8

Christians with little faith are very fearful. These group of Christians are afraid of everything. They are afraid of the unknown and what may happen or may not happen. They are afraid to take any risk, even if it will push them forward in life. In **Matthew 8:26**, the disciples were afraid that they will be drowned in the sea but all they had to do was to speak to Master Jesus. *Do not be afraid because Satan has been defeated! All you need to do is to use the name of Jesus.*

Christians with little faith are also doubters. They constantly doubt and their doubt prevents them from receiving their breakthroughs. Doubt is an enemy of faith. The word of God says in **James 1:6** that those who doubt or waver will not receive anything from Him. In Mark 14:31, Peter was walking on the sea following Jesus but as soon as he began to doubt, he began to sink.

A person with this kind of faith must put their trust in the firm foundation of God's immutable word. They must believe that no matter what the circumstance, God's word stands forever true.

Shipwrecked faith

Holding faith, and a good conscience; which some having put away CONCERNING FAITH HAVE MADE SHIPWRECK:

1 Timothy 1:19

A Christian who continues to live in sin and does not live according to their new nature in Christ is not holding faith and a good conscience. Good conscience is necessary for your faith to work to its full potential. For instance, some Christians do not have faith to pray because of the guilt of sin. Some even do not have the desire to go to church after they have fornicated in case the pastor preaches against fornication and their conscience pricks them. Having being a pastor for some time, I have noticed that when church members are living in sin, they do not come and say hello to you after church. They try to avoid the pastor as much as possible.

You will make a shipwreck of your faith in God if your conscience is not right. We must therefore pay particular attention to how we live our Christian lives in order to have a pure conscience. **1 Timothy 1:19** encourages us to have a good conscience while living a life of faith. My dear Christian sister, my dear Christian brother; you must hold your faith in a good conscience so that your faith will work fully for you.

Great Faith

And when Jesus was entered into Capernaum, there came unto him a centurion, beseeching him, And saying, Lord, my servant lieth at home sick of the palsy, grievously tormented.

And Jesus saith unto him, I will come and heal him. The centurion answered and said, Lord, I am not worthy that thou shouldest come under my roof: but speak the word only, and my servant shall be healed.

For I am a man under authority, having soldiers under me: and I say to this man, Go, and he goeth; and to another, Come, and he cometh; and to my servant, Do this, and he doeth it.

When Jesus heard it, he marvelled, and said to them that followed, Verily I say unto you, I HAVE NOT FOUND SO GREAT FAITH, no, not in Israel.

Matthew 8:5-10

A person who truly believes in the word of God has great faith just like the Centurion in the above scripture. Christians must believe that once the word of God has said it,. then it is final and needs no further discussion or argument. The Centurion said, *"Master just speak the word and my servant will be healed"*. ***He believed in the power of the word. He believed in the two edged sword, he believed in the engrafted word that is able to save our souls!***

Isaiah 55:10-11 tells us that the word of God shall never return to Him void, it shall be performed. In order to have great faith, you must believe in the word of God. The Centurion's servant was healed in the same hour the word was spoken by Jesus.

Strong Faith

He staggered not at the promise of God through unbelief; but was STRONG IN FAITH, giving glory to God;

And being fully persuaded that, what he had promised, he was able also to perform.

Romans 4:20-21

Strong faith knows no limits and knows no defeat. Nothing is impossible as far as a person with strong faith in Jesus is concerned. A believer with strong faith is never defeated because they knows that their God is bigger than any problem or situation they face. *With men it is impossible but with God, all things are possible!*

I once visited a brother in my church who was suffering from high blood pressure. He was so worried that he was not able to leave his house to come to church. So once Sunday, I gathered few of my shepherds and visited him at home. He said that his blood pressure was so high that the doctors thought he was about to die. After he had finished speaking, I read the scripture from **Mark 10:27** to him. *With men it is impossible, but with God, all things are possible!*

After saying this to him, I laid hands on him because the prayer of faith shall save the sick. Suddenly, the power of the Holy Ghost fell upon him and he began to shake uncontrollably as if he has been plugged into an electrical socket. After the prayer, I asked him if he had a machine that takes blood pressure in the house. He said yes. I said to him, "check your blood pressure now". To the glory of God, when he checked, his blood pressure had totally dropped.

The following day, he went to the doctor for a check-up. The doctor was amazed that his blood pressure had gone down. This was strong faith in operation. With strong faith, there is nothing like "it is worse" or "it cannot be solved". It is a persistent faith. With strong faith, all things are possible to a believer as it is with God. Like Abraham, strong faith does not stagger at the promises of God. With strong faith, you are fully persuaded that Almighty God will perform what He has promised.

Unfeigned faith

Now the end of the commandment is charity out of a pure heart, and of a good conscience, and OF FAITH UNFEIGNED:

1 Timothy 1:5

When I was growing up as a Christian, one of my greatest challenges was the pretence and hypocrisy in the church. I remember walking on the university campus and asking God "why do Christians pretend?" This was because of what I saw in the church. Christians were gossiping about each other and living a life different from what is portrayed in the church. Some Christians look like holy angels in the church and behave like demons outside the church. Apostle Paul said in the above scripture that our faith must be *unfeigned* or *sincere*. As a Christian, the life you live in darkness must be the same as the life you live in the church. In other words, your secret life must be the same as the life you live in the open. We must be sincere in our walk with the Lord.

Saving Faith

Both the blind man and the woman in the two passages of scriptures below needed deliverance and they received it by their actions. Your faith will save you if you take the right actions.

And it came to pass, that as he was come nigh unto Jericho, a certain blind man sat by the way side begging:

And hearing the multitude pass by, he asked what it meant. And they told him, that Jesus of Nazareth passeth by. And he cried, saying, Jesus, thou Son of David, have mercy on me.

And they which went before rebuked him, that he should hold his peace: but he cried so much the more, Thou Son of David, have mercy on me.

And Jesus stood, and commanded him to be brought unto him: and when he was come near, he asked him, Saying, What wilt thou that I shall do unto thee? And he said, Lord, that I may receive my sight. And Jesus said unto him, Receive thy sight: THY FAITH HATH SAVED THEE.

Luke 18:35-42

And Jesus answering said unto him, Simon, I have somewhat to say unto thee. And he saith, Master, say on. There was a certain creditor which had two debtors: the one owed five hundred pence, and the other fifty. And when they had nothing to pay, he frankly forgave them both. Tell me therefore, which of them will love him most?

Simon answered and said, I suppose that he, to whom he forgave most. And he said unto him, Thou hast rightly judged. And he turned to the woman, and said unto Simon, Seest thou this woman? I entered into thine house, thou gavest me no water for my feet: but she hath washed my feet with tears, and wiped them with the hairs of her head. Thou gavest me no kiss: but this woman since the time I came in hath not ceased to kiss my feet. My head with oil thou didst not anoint: but this woman hath anointed my feet with ointment.

Wherefore I say unto thee, Her sins, which are many, are forgiven; for she loved much: but to whom little is forgiven, the same loveth little. And he said unto her, Thy sins are forgiven. And they that sat at meat with him began to say within themselves, Who is this that forgiveth sins also? And he said to the woman, THY FAITH HATH SAVED THEE; go in peace.

Luke 7:40-50

The word "Saved" in both of these scriptures has the same meaning. It means *to deliver, preserve, protect, to heal* and *to make whole*. Take the actions that will preserve your life, the actions that will protect you and the actions that will enable you to receive your healing! A church member once said to me, "Pastor, once I decided to give it all to Jesus, everything is now working for me". Unless you surrender totally to Jesus, you are not going to experience the fullness of His blessing. The woman in **Luke 7** surrendered all to Jesus. She gave up all the secret boyfriends she had and she was delivered by her faith.

The Door of Faith

The door of faith is an opportunity that the Lord gives to allow someone to receive the gospel. We must recognise these opportunities and make good use of them. Just like the doors opened for the disciples to preach in Perga, Attalia, Antioch and so forth, doors will also open to every believer and we must identify and preach the gospel to the lost.

The door may open for you to preach to your dad, mum, friends, work colleagues and relatives. It is impossible for you to be my friend and not hear the gospel. Even work colleagues cannot escape the gospel if they come into contact with me. I am always looking for the door of faith in other to preach the gospel to the lost.

I remember a gentleman who I was trying to preach to and he would never listen to me. But when his father died, I realised that it was a door of faith for me to preach to him. He was born into a very rich family but when the father became sick, they realised that the riches could not save him. The father was seen by the best doctors in the best hospitals yet he still died. This was a door of opportunity to preach the gospel. This gentleman is now a born again Christian filled with the Holy Ghost. He finally realised that Jesus is the only answer.

I have preached at funeral services because the people who are dead have departed but those who are alive still have the opportunity to receive salvation. There is no repentance in the grave. Funerals are not just a time for crying and mourning but also a time to ponder about what will happen after death. Funeral services are a sure door of faith to preach the gospel.

And when they had preached the word in Perga, they went down into Attalia:

And thence sailed to Antioch, from whence they had been recommended to the grace of God for the work which they fulfilled.

And when they were come, and had gathered the church together, they rehearsed all that God had done with them, and how he had opened the DOOR OF FAITH unto the Gentiles.
Acts 14:25-27

Full of Faith

You must be a Christian who is full of faith. A person's faith is exhibited by their actions and sayings. This is noticeable as it can be seen by others and it is infectious. You can change the mood of an atmosphere just by being full of faith. A sad atmosphere can become a joyous atmosphere by your faith. In other words, your faith can affect your surroundings. Most Christians who are always moody and of a sad countenance often lack faith. They create a bad atmosphere wherever they find themselves. *From today, I see your faith affecting your environment and changing the very atmosphere in which you live!* Be a man or woman who is full of faith like Stephen and the rest of the faith people mentioned in the scripture below.

And the saying pleased the whole multitude: and they chose Stephen, a man FULL OF FAITH and of the Holy Ghost, and Philip, and Prochorus, and Nicanor, and Timon, and Parmenas, and Nicolas a proselyte of Antioch:

Acts 6:5

Exceeding Growing Faith

Your faith must grow. It must not remain the same as the faith you received at salvation. Through tests, trials and experiences, you must use the word of God to pass through those seasons of your life. Your faith will grow exceedingly as mentioned in **2 Thessalonians 1:3**.

We are bound to thank God always for you, brethren, as it is meet, because that YOUR FAITH GROWETH EXCEEDINGLY, and the charity of every one of you all toward each other aboundeth;

2 Thessalonians 1:3

Dead Faith

Your faith must have a corresponding action. It must cause you to do something. If you are believing God for a husband, you must go down on your knees and pray. After you have prayed, you must also make an effort to look nice!

This is the corresponding action due to your faith in God that He is able to provide you with a husband. In other words, your faith is a dead faith if it has no work to show. Christians who do not partake in any activities in their local church have dead faith. Surely, if you say you have faith in God, the corresponding action is that you will want to do something for Him.

Watch out for Christians who are always asking God to do something for them and never do anything in return. I have realised that people who come to church to serve God and people who come to church because they are looking for a husband, wife, money, job or help from the church are very different. Those who come with the agenda of looking for material things do not stay once that need is fulfilled.

The opposite is also true! There are also those who leave if the need is not fulfilled immediately. I once conducted a baby dedication for a couple. After the baby dedication, they left the church. I have seen countless number of Christians who have left churches after they received what they were looking for. These are believers with dead faith.

EVEN SO FAITH, IF IT HATH NOT WORKS, IS DEAD, being alone.

James 2:17

Wavering Faith

But let him ask in faith, nothing wavering. For he that WAVERETH is like a wave of the sea driven with the wind and tossed.

James 1:6

The waves of the sea are very unstable and so is a Christian whose faith wavers. Today he is full of faith but tomorrow his faith is dead. A Christian with this kind of faith lives according to the trend of the day. When things are good, he is full of faith. But when things are bad, his faith dies. Your faith must stand no matter what circumstances you face.

Faith that Overcomes the World

As I mentioned in the earlier chapters of this book, you cannot stand as a Christian without faith. There are so many hindrances in this world that can quench your faith and the only way to overcome such hindrances in your world is overcoming faith. There is a certain faith that overcomes the world by ensuring that we are always victorious. *I see you having an overcoming faith in Jesus name!*

If you believe that Jesus is the Son of God, you have a world overcoming faith! You shall certainly overcome the issues and problems of this life! As the saying goes, with Jesus in the vessel, you shall smile at the storm.

For whatsoever is born of God OVERCOMETH THE WORLD: and this is the victory that OVERCOMETH THE WORLD, even our faith.

Who is he that OVERCOMETH THE WORLD, but he that believeth that Jesus is the Son of God?

1 John 5:4-5

Failing Faith

Satan will bring troubles your way but I am encouraging you just like Jesus encouraged Peter that your faith must not fail. Have a daily prayer life so in times of trouble, you will stand. *I see you standing in spite of all the issues in your life! You will overcome because you are an overcomer!* As the Bible says in **Romans 8:37**, we are more than conquerors.

And the Lord said, Simon, Simon, behold, Satan hath desired to have you, that he may sift you as wheat:

But I have prayed for thee, that thy FAITH FAIL NOT: and when thou art converted, strengthen thy brethren.

Luke 22:31-32

Increasing Faith

Your faith can increase and it must increase. You can ask the Lord to increase your faith in a particular situation that is proving difficult to handle. Sometimes things happen in our lives which seem beyond our faith but if you take it to the Lord in prayer, He will increase your faith to overcome it. When the disciples looked at what Jesus was saying in **Luke 17**, they could only ask Him to increase their faith.

And the apostles said unto the Lord, INCREASE OUR FAITH.

Luke 17:5

Faith Made Perfect by Works

A faith made perfect by works is a matured faith. A matured faith exhibits the types of faith which are, **the measure of faith, the gift of faith and the fruit of faith**. Endeavour to get your faith perfect in Christ Jesus by putting faith to work.

Seest thou how faith wrought with his works, and by works was FAITH MADE PERFECT?

James 2:22

Rich Faith

I truly think that the poorest countries in this world have more faith than the richer countries. The poor people often live in deprived places and rely on God for everything from good health, clothing to shelter and food. These people are rich in faith because faith is their currency for survival. A true believer must be rich in faith and must have total dependency on God no matter which part of the world you live in. God is our provider. He gives us the grace and the power to make wealth. He heals us and provides us with our daily bread.

Hearken, my beloved brethren, Hath not God chosen the poor of this world RICH IN FAITH, and heirs of the kingdom which he hath promised to them that love him?

James 2:5

And now abideth faith, hope, charity, these three; but the greatest of these is charity.

1 Corinthians 13:13

Chapter 14

Pillars of Faith

I will define a pillar as that invisible part of a building that holds the building together. Without pillars, a building will collapse. Usually it is placed in the four corners when building a house. This is to give the building a solid foundation and strength. What I call the pillars of faith are therefore the forces that make faith works. Faith by itself cannot work and will not work effectively without these forces. These forces or PILLARS are therefore necessary to see the full manifestation of faith.

There are three main pillars of faith and without these, it is impossible for faith to work. These pillars are HOPE, LOVE and PATIENCE. They form a three-fold cord that cannot be broken. Faith coupled with hope, love and patience are inseparable.

And now abideth faith, hope, charity, these three; but the greatest of these is charity.

1 Corinthians 13:13

That ye be not slothful, but followers of them who through faith and patience inherit the promises.

Hebrews 6:12

Hope

The word "Hope" is the belief that *something expected will happen* or *it is possible of happening or occurring*. Apostle Paul said in **Philippians 1:20** that he had an earnest expectation in hope that he will not be ashamed that Christ will be magnified in his body.

Hope gives the believer an expectation of something to look forward to. Without hope, there can be no faith as there will be nothing to believe God for. Hope is therefore the object of faith.

Who against HOPE believed in HOPE, that he might become the father of many nations, according to that which was spoken, So shall thy seed be.

And being not weak in faith, he considered not his own body now dead, when he was about an hundred years old, neither yet the deadness of Sara's womb:

He staggered not at the promise of God through unbelief; but was strong in faith, giving glory to God;

And being fully persuaded that, what he had promised, he was able also to perform.

Romans 4:18-21

For there is hope of a tree, if it be cut down, that it will sprout again, and that the tender branch thereof will not cease.

Job 14:7

The word of God in **Romans 4:18** states that *"against hope, Abraham believed in hope"*. His hope gave him an expectation of what the Lord had promised him, that in his seed shall all the nations of the earth be blessed. Abraham and Sarah were both very old. In fact, the word of God says that Abraham did not consider the weakness of his body nor the deadness of Sarah's womb. It was hopeless for both of them to have any expectation of having a child. For Sarah to conceive was an impossibility. ***Yet Abraham had hope and an expectation that to men it is impossible, but to God all things are possible!***

The word of God and its promises are the foundations of hope. **Colossians 1:27** declares that Christ in us is the hope of glory. In other words, for the believer no condition is hopeless. You can hope in the promises of God; that is it possible according to His word. The promises of God are *yea* and *amen* and they will surely come to pass. We have a promise that by His stripes we are healed in **Isaiah 53:5** and in **1 Peter 2:24**. We have a promise that our God will supply all our needs in **Philippians 4:19**. There are countless other promises concerning every area of our lives in the word of God. We must stand on them to receive our blessings.

Now, because I have hope, I can have the faith to pray and seek God about any particular situation. Hope is therefore the force that drives faith. ***Your hope makes you act on your faith***. Your hope makes you put the word into action. It gives you the desire and the drive to earnestly activate the word of God through faith.

The psalmist said in **Psalm 42:5**, *"why are you cast down oh my soul, hope thou in the Lord"*. The word of God also says in **Job 22:29** *"When men are cast down, then thou shalt say, There is lifting up;*

and he shall save the humble person". No Christian whose hope is in the Lord will ever commit suicide. Therefore, hope is the remedy for depression and suicidal decisions. When you are on the train, you often here the announcement that there is a person under the train. Ask yourself, why would a person take their own life? It is because they think there is no hope for them.

I tell you the truth, there is surely hope for you! If there was hope for the dry bones in Ezekiel 37, then there is hope for you! If there is hope that the dead can rise again, then there is hope for you! There is hope for your healing! There is hope for your conception! There is hope for your blessing! And there is hope for your promotion!

Thank God for Jesus that our hope is not built on sinking sand. Our hope is built on the Solid Rock which cannot be destroyed and it never dies. Jesus is our hope! Hope and faith are inseparable. You must have hope for something in other to have faith to bring it to pass. Your faith cannot flourish without hope.

Love

For in Jesus Christ neither circumcision availeth any thing, nor uncircumcision; but faith which WORKETH BY LOVE.
Galatians 5:6

According to the word of God, our faith will not work without love. This scripture explains why so many Christians do not receive answers to their prayers. There is no love in their hearts for anyone apart from themselves. When you are this type of person, no matter how much you pray and fast or go to church, your faith will not work for you. We must therefore pray to the Father to give us His kind of love that is unconditional.

They are of the world: therefore speak they of the world, and the world heareth them.

We are of God: he that knoweth God heareth us; he that is not of God heareth not us. Hereby know we the spirit of truth, and the spirit of error.

Beloved, let us love one another: for love is of God; and every one that loveth is born of God, and knoweth God. He that loveth not knoweth not God; for God is love.

1 John 4:5-8

Firstly, we must have love for God Himself. Our love for God will cause us to spend time in prayer and in worship with Him. This love causes you to read and study the scriptures. It is this love that makes you go to church to fellowship.

Most Christians say they love God but they do not give to the Lord. The cardinal sign of love is giving. You should be willing to give all that you have to the Lord. The Lord first loved us with an unconditional love. **Romans 5:8** tells us that while we were still sinners, God sent His son Jesus to die for all mankind. This is the demonstration of true love. God gave to the world a costly gift by sacrificing His beloved son to redeem and to rescue us from the claws of the enemy.

For God so loved the world, that he gave his only begotten Son, that whosoever believeth in him should not perish, but have everlasting life.

John 3:16

If a man says to a woman "I love you", but is always taking without giving, it is a clear sign that this man looking for something else other than love. The reason why there is a lot of divorce in the world and even in the churches is because people are marrying for selfish reasons. They marry because of what they can get, whether it's for a certain kind of passport or because the other person is rich. This selfish nature of mankind has damaged a lot of marriages.

Love is the essential ingredient in marriage. It causes husbands and wives to love each other for better for worse. When you love something, you will give yourself wholly to it, whether it be marriage or worship to God.

You cannot say you truly love God and yet you keep your time, your energy and your money from Him. From today, give willing and cheerfully when an offering is being taken in church. Pay your tithes as a sign of your love for God. You must love God to even have the confidence to ask Him for your needs. If you do not have that confidence in Him, your faith will not work.

The word of God also tells us that you cannot say you love God whom you have not seen and hate your brother or next door neighbour whom you can see. If you do not have love for others, your faith will not work. Some people do not love anyone apart from themselves and they exhibit this behaviour even in the house of God. God requires us to love each other.

If a man say, I love God, and hateth his brother, HE IS A LIAR: for he that loveth not his brother whom he hath seen, how can he love God whom he hath not seen?

1 John 4:20

Christians and individuals who hate another human being created in the image of God do not have true love in their heart. In fact, the word of God compares you to a liar and a murderer for hating your neighbour. Forgiveness is therefore an important sign of love. If you love your brother, you will forgive him of any wrong done to you, no matter how bad it is to you. God said that if you do not forgive men their sins, He will never forgive you your sins. And when you stand to pray and you have something against anyone, your prayers will not be answered. So it is for our own good to love others.

We know that we have passed from death unto life, because we love the brethren. He that loveth not his brother abideth in death.

Whosoever hateth his brother is a MURDERER: and ye know that no murderer hath eternal life abiding in him.

1 John 3:14-15

When a poor man asks you for money, do not say "no, he is going to use it to drink alcohol". Your duty is to just give if you can. As for what the person uses the money for, it is none of your business. The Lord loves those who consider the poor and He watches over them just as He watches over the poor. Of course you cannot give to all the poor in the world but give to the poor when the Lord touches your heart to give. When a certain compassion comes on you for the beggar by the roadside, heed to the voice of God and bless the poor. Some people do not have compassion for the poor at all and they must pray for it.

He that hath a bountiful eye shall be blessed; for he giveth of his bread to the poor.

Proverbs 22:9

Blessed is he that considereth the poor: the LORD will deliver him in time of trouble.

The LORD will preserve him, and keep him alive; and he shall be blessed upon the earth: and thou wilt not deliver him unto the will of his enemies.

The LORD will strengthen him upon the bed of languishing: thou wilt make all his bed in his sickness.

Psalm 41:-1-3

All the blessings in the above scriptures shall happen to you and make your faith work if you consider the poor. Do not treat the poor unjustly. Love the poor like you love the rich man.

The Lord loves the lost souls. In actual fact, God says that the son of man came to seek and to save the lost.

For the Son of man is come to seek and to save that which was lost.

Luke 19:10

The main reason why Jesus came to this world was to ensure that no human being goes to hell. God did not create hell for mankind but He created it for satan and his followers. God desires that all men be saved and come to know the Lord Jesus Christ.

Who will have all men to be saved, and to come unto the knowledge of the truth.

1 Timothy 2:4

If we say we love God, then we must love the lost souls. He came to shed His blood for them and to pull them out of the pit of hell. That is why He commanded us to preach the gospel to the entire world.

And he said unto them, Go ye into all the world, and preach the gospel to every creature.

He that believeth and is baptized shall be saved; but he that believeth not shall be damned.

Mark 16:15-16

Go ye therefore, and teach all nations, baptizing them in the name of the Father, and of the Son, and of the Holy Ghost:

Teaching them to observe all things whatsoever I have commanded you: and, lo, I am with you alway, even unto the end of the world. Amen.

Matthew 28:19-20

Personal evangelism is another sign that you love God and that you are ready to do His will. Tell others about Christ. Witness to your friends, relatives, work colleagues and acquaintances. We must witness daily to the people we meet every day because people are dying everyday. It is your love for God that will cause you to evangelise.

If ye love me, keep my commandments.

John 14:15

Patience

Patience is the third pillar of faith. Without patience, frustration sets in which quenches faith. And when faith is quenched, the flesh takes control and leads us to try and solve the problems ourselves instead of depending on God to take charge. But the word of God states that we should be followers of them who through **faith and patience**, inherit the promises.

That ye be not slothful, but followers of them who through FAITH AND PATIENCE inherit the promises.

Hebrews 6:12

Abraham had waited a long time for a child and it looked as if the promise of God was delayed. Frustration set in and he had a child with Haggai his servant. But this was not the original plan of God for his life. The plan of God was that Abraham will have his own child through his wife Sarah.

Patience is therefore the pillar that sustains faith. Where there is patience, faith never quenches! Where there is patience, a believer never gives up! Where there is patience, the believer seeks God persistently and continuously until they receive an answer!

Patience produces the ability to wait and not give up. A patient Christian is a victorious person because they are always on the winning side. Faith that is not tried will not survive the trials of life. When faith is tested and tried, patience is produced. The word of God says in **James 1:4** that when patience has finished its work, you will be perfect and wanting nothing. Therefore faith sustained with patience will produce a perfect result.

I beseech you my fellow believers, do not complain and murmur when your blessings seem to delay. Keep seeking God! Keep praying persistently and surely, you shall receive your blessings! If faith is not tried, we can never tell whether we truly believe or not. Even Jesus was tested and proved for His faith. Abraham was tested, Daniel was tested, and Joseph was tried and tested. All these people became very great in the sight of men and in the sight of God.

You see, a tested and tried faith produces patience and strong faith in a believer. That is why the word of God says that you must count it all joy when you fall into diverse trials and temptations. *May you stand the test of time because of your patience!*

I marvel at Christians who stop going to church because their prayers have not been answered. Some even cut themselves away from God and jump back into the world. But we must be able to stand and say like Apostle Paul, "what shall separate us from the love of God, shall tribulation, nakedness, hunger?" We must answer with an emphatic "NO, NOTHING shall separate me from His love." For in all these tests we remain more than conquerors. This is patience in action and we must follow by example.

He that spared not his own Son, but delivered him up for us all, how shall he not with him also freely give us all things?

Who shall lay any thing to the charge of God's elect? It is God that justifieth. Who is he that condemneth? It is Christ that died, yea rather, that is risen again, who is even at the right hand of God, who also maketh intercession for us. Who shall separate us from the love of Christ? shall tribulation, or distress, or persecution, or famine, or nakedness, or peril, or sword?

As it is written, For thy sake we are killed all the day long; we are accounted as sheep for the slaughter. Nay, in all these things we are more than conquerors through him that loved us.

For I am persuaded, that neither death, nor life, nor angels, nor principalities, nor powers, nor things present, nor things to come, Nor height, nor depth, nor any other creature, shall be able to separate us from the love of God, which is in Christ Jesus our Lord.

Romans 8:32-39

And yet I say unto you, That even Solomon in all his glory was not arrayed like one of these. Wherefore, if God so clothe the grass of the field, which to day is, and to morrow is cast into the oven, shall he not much more clothe you, O ye of little faith? Therefore take no thought, saying, What shall we eat? or, What shall we drink? or, Wherewithal shall we be clothed?

Matthew 6:29-31

Chapter 15

Enemies of Faith

The enemies of faith are forces that fight against your faith. Their presence in your life negates your faith. We must therefore watch out for these forces and get rid of them. They are weapons used by the enemy to ensure that believers do not receive answers to their prayers. It keeps them in bondage to not have enough faith to possess their possessions.

Fear

Forasmuch then as the children are partakers of flesh and blood, he also himself likewise took part of the same; that through death he might destroy him that had the power of death, that is, the devil;

And deliver them who through fear of death were all their lifetime subject to bondage.

Hebrews 2:14-15

According to the passage of scripture above, fear can keep people in bondage throughout their whole lifetime. Anything that keeps you in bondage takes away your freedom and your liberty.

But we must stand in the liberty because Jesus has made us free and we should not be entangled again with the yoke of bondage. We must constantly cast out fear and allow our hearts to be filled with faith.

Fear is the opposite of faith and when it is present in a believer's life, it nullifies faith. It is one of the first demons sent by satan into people's lives in order to weaken them. When a Christian is struck with the demon of fear, other bigger demons are then sent to finish the work of satan in that person.

The word of God tells us **2 Timothy 1:7** that God has not given us a spirit of fear but of power, love and of a sound mind. This scripture tells us that fear is a spirit and this spirit does not come from God Almighty. Fear is the spirit of satan that operates in the lives of people.

When someone is diagnosed with HIV, just the fear of having that kind of disease alone kills the person faster. But a person of faith who believes that God is able to heal and to save, has hope which keeps them alive longer. They may even be healed if they have enough faith to receive their healing. Fearful people never receive their breakthrough because they do not have the boldness and the faith to go for what belongs to them. They are subject to bondage their whole life.

But I see you breaking out! I see you overcoming the spirit of fear to receive what belongs to you! I bind the spirit of fear in your life and I cast that evil spirit out right now in the name of Jesus! Receive boldness! Receive power! May you have a sound mind in the name of Jesus! You will not die, you will live! You will marry!

You will finish your education! You will have children! You will have all that satan has said you will not have! Do not be afraid, believe in the Lord God Almighty!

The good news is that we have not received the spirit of bondage. We have received the Spirit of adoption! And this same Holy Spirit that we have received instead of the spirit of fear, liberates us from every bondage! For where the Spirit of God is Lord, there is liberty. For this cause, Jesus Christ was raised up to destroy the works of darkness, which is the devil.

Mediate on the scriptures below and allow them to minister to you. Receive your liberty that comes from the most High God!

For ye have not received the spirit of bondage again to fear; but ye have received the Spirit of adoption, whereby we cry, Abba, Father.

Romans 8:15

Now the Lord is that Spirit: and where the Spirit of the Lord is, there is liberty.

2 Corinthians 3:17

He that committeth sin is of the devil; for the devil sinneth from the beginning. For this purpose the Son of God was manifested, that he might destroy the works of the devil.

1 John 3:8

Worry

Be CAREFUL for nothing; but in every thing by prayer and supplication with thanksgiving let your requests be made known unto God.

Philippians 4:6

And yet I say unto you, That even Solomon in all his glory was not arrayed like one of these.

Wherefore, if God so clothe the grass of the field, which to day is, and to morrow is cast into the oven, shall he not much more clothe you, O ye of little faith?

Therefore TAKE NO THOUGHT, saying, What shall we eat? or, What shall we drink? or, Wherewithal shall we be clothed?

Matthew 6:29-31

The word "careful" in **Philippians 4:6**, comes from the Greek word "merimnao", which means to *take thought*. Now, it may interest you to know that the same Greek word "merimnao", is used for the word *"thought"* in **Matthew 6:31.**

I want to point out to you that worry is a demon that works on the mind of a person. This demon works in conjunction with the demons of fear and doubt to drive a person to a state of hopelessness. The end result of this demon is that a Christian becomes faithless and begins to contemplate of committing suicide. That is why the word of God encourages us not to worry about tomorrow.

The Oxford Dictionary defines "anxiety" as *a state* or *feeling*, and defines the adjective "anxious" as *a state of feeling worried or nervous*. It may interest you to know that the dictionary also gives synonyms of both "anxiety" and "anxious" as *worry, fear, doubts, fretful, disturbed, and nervous* and the list goes on.

Before a person becomes anxious or worried, the demon of fear comes upon the person and once this happens, the demon of worry follows suit. Now the person begins to process these thoughts of worry over and over again about something that they cannot solve. I call this 'opening the devil's bible' because in the devil's book is worry, headache, depression and suicide. Once the devil has been able to get you into this state of mind, he is now able to finish you. He does not stop there but he is also able to use people who are very close to you who do not believe in God to speak more doubt into your life.

I have often heard people in this state tell me that they no longer believe in God because they have tried God and God was not able to help them. But this is exactly what the demons of fear, worry and doubt aim to achieve in your life. You see, satan operates on the power of suggestion. He suggests bad things to your mind and as you ponder and ponder over such negative thoughts, he is able to accomplish his plans in your life. Never allow this to happen to you! Flush out every negative thought that comes into your mind for the weapons of our warfare are not carnal.

For though we walk in the flesh, we do not war after the flesh:

(For the weapons of our warfare are not carnal, but mighty through God to the pulling down of strong holds;)

Casting down imaginations, and every high thing that exalteth itself against the knowledge of God, and bringing into captivity every thought to the obedience of Christ;

2 Corinthians 10:3-5

Pastors, when a person is in this state of mind, counselling and talking will not help. Just enter into your closet and pray to break this evil power over the person in the name of Jesus. *For this cause, Christ was raised up to destroy the works of darkness!*

I remember when one of my church members, who was then a growing Christian, went into this state. The devil drove this person to this state of mind until the person became depressed, constantly crying and eventually giving up on God. But I went into my closet and battled with satan for the soul of this church member. To the glory of God, this church member is now settled in the kingdom of God.

Worrying is sin because many of the things that Christians worry about, only God can solve them. We must therefore trust and hope in the Lord and carry our burdens to Him. Did He not says in **Matthew 11:28** that come unto me with your burden and I will give you rest? Did He also not say in **1 Peter 5:7** that cast all your cares upon Him because He cares for you? Now read these scriptures carefully and meditate upon them and allow them to settle in your heart.

Come unto me, all ye that labour and are heavy laden, and I will give you rest.

Matthew 11:28

Casting all your care upon him; for he careth for you.

1 Peter 5:7

Cast thy burden upon the LORD, and he shall sustain thee: he shall never suffer the righteous to be moved.

Psalm 55:22

Remember that if the devil is able to capture your thoughts, then he will be able to destroy you. Never allow negative thoughts to come to your mind. Yes, flashes may occur to your mind, but cast them out by rejecting them in Jesus name.

Doubt

For verily I say unto you, That whosoever shall say unto this mountain, Be thou removed, and be thou cast into the sea; and shall not doubt in his heart, but shall believe that those things which he saith shall come to pass; he shall have whatsoever he saith.

Mark 11:23

The above passage of scripture shows us that doubt takes place in the heart and not in the mind. So if your mind thinks that you will not receive what you have prayed for and your heart says the opposite then you will have it. You shall receive what you prayed for if doubt is not in your heart.

To "doubt" means *to stagger* and *to hesitate* in your heart. It means you are staggering and hesitating at the promises of God. It also means *to waver*. In **James 1:5**, anyone who doubts will not receive anything from the Lord. This makes doubt an enemy of faith. In actual fact, it is one of the deadliest enemies of faith because as soon as doubt occurs, you can not receive your blessings.

In order to overcome doubt, we must have the heart of a child in that a child believes everything. We must have total trust and confidence in the promises of God. We must believe that whatever has come out of the mouth of the Lord shall be established for God is not a man that He should lie.

God is not a man, that he should lie; neither the son of man, that he should repent: hath he said, and shall he not do it? or hath he spoken, and shall he not make it good?

Numbers 23:19

Let every man be a liar and let God be true for the promises of God in him are *Yea* and *Amen*.

For all the promises of God in him are yea, and in him Amen, unto the glory of God by us.

2 Corinthians 1:20

We must therefore have total assurance in the word of God. It has been tried and tested over several generations. It has been scrutinised and examined in diverse ways and it has stood the test of time. As **Psalm 119:89 states**, *"Forever oh God thy word is settled in heaven."*

Fear, worry and doubt are demons of faith. Do not entertain them. Cast them out of your thoughts and you will live a victorious life!

Laziness

Laziness is the next enemy of faith. Laziness kills faith. As I said earlier on, faith demands action and doings. But I have come to realise that lazy people do not experience the blessings of faith because their faith simple does not work.

That ye be not slothful, but followers of them who through faith and patience inherit the promises.
Hebrews 6:12

You can see in the above scripture that you will receive the promise of God if you are not slothful which means if you are not lazy. Laziness is a spirit that has the power to negate the faith of people. It prevents them from moving forwards.

A lazy person does not want to work. They sit at one place and expect the Lord to shower manna from Heaven on them. But I announce to you that you must act on your faith for abundant blessings. Some Christians are so lazy. They do not want to work and just live on government benefit all their lives. Why then do you cry about not having this or that in your life? Lift yourself up and do something and allow the Lord to bless the work of your hands. Give an offering, sow a seed for your breakthrough, go for prayer meetings, do some fasting and see if you will not receive your blessings.

The fact that you are not doing anything to activate your faith shows why you are in such a terrible situation. From today, begin to move! As you begin to do so, you will see results for faith without works is a dead faith.

What You See and What You Hear

What you see and what you hear can greatly affect your faith. I was once trying to encourage a lady about marriage but I soon realised that this lady had no faith in the area of marriage. She had actually become allergic to that topic. She began to explain what she has seen in her family and how the father has abused the mother over and over again. She has seen the mother beaten, assaulted, raped and cut with knives by the father. According to this lady, she saw the mother crying constantly and the father actually became the mother's prayer topic. Anytime the mother prayed, the topic was about the father. So she said to me, "how can I marry if this is what happens in marriage?" "To be in bondage for the rest of my life is not my portion". This poor lady's faith was greatly affected by what she had seen over the years. She had no desire to marry, and as far as she was concerned, faith in this area had been greatly damaged by the parents.

In the Old Testament, Moses sent some spies to go and spy the Promised Land that God has given to the children of Israel. But when they returned from spying the land, the majority of the spies brought a bad report to Moses because of what they had seen on the land. They said we are not able to go up against them because the people on the land are stronger than us.

Although God had promised to give them this land, the spies' faith has been affected by what they saw on the land and they could not believe that with men it is impossible but with God all things are possible. Be careful what you hear and what you see.

But Caleb who was one of the spies brought a good report to the people. He arose and silenced the others and said, "let us go up at once and possess the land for we are well able to overcome it". This is faith in action. Caleb was not moved by what he saw on the land. He was not moved by the great walls and the giants on the land. He was moved by His faith in Jesus. Jesus said, *"Take heed what you hear"* in **Mark 4:24**.

And they returned from searching of the land after forty days. And they went and came to Moses, and to Aaron, and to all the congregation of the children of Israel, unto the wilderness of Paran, to Kadesh; and brought back word unto them, and unto all the congregation, and shewed them the fruit of the land.

And they told him, and said, We came unto the land whither thou sentest us, and surely it floweth with milk and honey; and this is the fruit of it. Nevertheless the people be strong that dwell in the land, and the cities are walled, and very great: and moreover we saw the children of Anak there.

The Amalekites dwell in the land of the south: and the Hittites, and the Jebusites, and the Amorites, dwell in the mountains: and the Canaanites dwell by the sea, and by the coast of Jordan.

And Caleb stilled the people before Moses, and said, Let us go up at once, and possess it; for we are well able to overcome it. But the men that went up with him said, We be not able to go up against the people; for they are stronger than we.

And they brought up an evil report of the land which they had searched unto the children of Israel, saying, The land, through

which we have gone to search it, is a land that eateth up the inhabitants thereof; and all the people that we saw in it are men of a great stature.

And there we saw the giants, the sons of Anak, which come of the giants: and we were in our own sight as grasshoppers, and so we were in their sight.

Numbers 13:25-33

Separate yourself from people who are always saying negative things with their mouths and are never positive. Stay in a positive environment where your faith is always empowered to move forth. Do not be moved by what you see for we walk by faith and not by sight.

Pride

Pride is a type of demonic spirit that can greatly hinder your faith. Proud people think that going to church is too low for them. Some are in church and they are too proud to even speak in tongues. Pride is what is affecting most Christians today. They are too proud to give offering and to pay tithes. They are even too proud to heed to the instruction of the man of God to receive their breakthrough. Pride was the demon that nearly caused Naaman the king to miss his blessing had it not been for good advice from a servant. When the man of God instructed Naaman to dip himself seven times in the river Jordan in order to receive his healing, he was annoyed just like most people in church today. At the mention of offering or a seed to receive a breakthrough, they get angry.

God will not do things the way you expect Him to do it for you. He does things differently and in His own way. **Isaiah 55:8** tells us that His thoughts are not our thoughts. Naaman thought that the prophet would have asked him to do something extraordinary in order to receive his healing. We do not like simple things, we like complicated stuff. That is how most people get into all sorts of trouble.

I once had a couple attend our church. During one of our services, I prayed for them and they fell under the power of God. I later heard that this couple had decided not to attend the church again saying that they cannot be bothered with "this falling down thing". Well, if you are running away from the Holy Spirit then you will never go to any good church because any good church will be full of the power and demonstration of the Holy Spirit. Their pride pushed them out of the church. Naaman finally heeded to the man of God and he was healed because he put his pride aside.

And it was so, when Elisha the man of God had heard that the king of Israel had rent his clothes, that he sent to the king, saying, Wherefore hast thou rent thy clothes? let him come now to me, and he shall know that there is a prophet in Israel.

So Naaman came with his horses and with his chariot, and stood at the door of the house of Elisha. And Elisha sent a messenger unto him, saying, Go and wash in Jordan seven times, and thy flesh shall come again to thee, and thou shalt be clean.

But Naaman was wroth, and went away, and said, Behold, I thought, He will surely come out to me, and stand, and call on the name of the LORD his God, and strike his hand over the place, and recover the leper.

Are not Abana and Pharpar, rivers of Damascus, better than all the waters of Israel? may I not wash in them, and be clean?

So he turned and went away in a rage. And his servants came near, and spake unto him, and said, My father, if the prophet had bid thee do some great thing, wouldest thou not have done it? how much rather then, when he saith to thee, Wash, and be clean?

Then went he down, and dipped himself seven times in Jordan, according to the saying of the man of God: and his flesh came again like unto the flesh of a little child, and he was clean.

2 Kings 5:8-14

Lay aside your pride and allow God to help you. Believe in God and believe also in the man of God that God is using to bless you. Never be angry in church because an offering is being taken for a particular cause. Humble yourself and you will receive more grace and blessing from the Lord.

Even so faith, if it hath not works, is dead, being alone.

James 2:17

Chapter 16

Building your Faith

The word of God is the word of faith. Therefore the more of the word you have in you, the more your faith grows. As a Christian, you must do all you can to get the word of God into your very being. Give time to the word and read your Bible every day. We eat physical food to grow physically but in order to build your faith, you need the word of God.

The Word of God

The word of God encourages us to feed on the word that we may grow. The Bible also says in **Matthew 4:4**, that man does not live by bread alone, but by every word that proceeds out of the mouth of God.

But what saith it? The word is nigh thee, even in thy mouth, and in thy heart: that is, the word of faith, which we preach;
Romans 10:8

Faith comes by hearing and hearing by the word of God. Which also means that faith can only increase by the word of God. Without the word of God, faith does not grow at all. What then must a Christian do to build their faith?

There are several ways that a Christian can get the word of God. You can get the word of God in your spirit by reading the Bible every blessed day. But reading the Bible alone is not enough. You must also learn how to study the Bible using the various Bible tools such as a Concordance which contains the Hebrew and Greek meanings of the words in the Bible. The Bible was originally written in the Hebrew and the Greek so it is necessary to get the original meanings of the words in the scriptures in order not to misinterpret the word of God. You will also need a good dictionary and a good Bible. Bibles such as Dake's Annotated Reference Bible and Thompson's Chain Reference Bibles are very useful for studying the word of God.

Another way of feeding your faith and building it with the word is by investing in your faith. Get anointed Christian books written by great men and women of God. Books written by anointed people of God can explain scriptures in a way that you might otherwise not understand on your own. As you read you shall get to know more scriptures, to understand them and be able to apply them to everyday life.

I have invested so much in books. I have read countless number of books from Bishop Dag Heward-Mills, Pastor Benny Hinn and Rev. Kenneth E Hagin to name a few. I almost have a bookshop at home because I started buying and reading anointed Christian books immediately I became born again. I still continue to buy and read such anointed books. You can read books on various topics like The Blood, the Holy Spirit, Baptism, Growing Up Spiritually and so forth. Spend money and build your faith.

Furthermore, through anointed audio preaching and video messages, you can greatly increase your faith. Faith increases as you listen and faith also increases as you hear. This is because faith comes by hearing and hearing by the word of God. Instead of listening to radio and watching useless programmes on the television, you can listen to anointed preaching messages and watch preaching videos. Once again, spend money on these for your own sake.

The final way you can build your faith is one of the most important ways of building your faith. You must fellowship regularly. Do not stay at home when service is going on. Find a good Bible believing church where the word of God is taught and be a faithful attendee. Sit under the feet of your pastor and allow him to teach you the word of God as he is led by the Spirit of God. By receiving the word, Sunday after Sunday and weekday after weekday, your faith will catapult. Never remove yourself from christian fellowship.

Not forsaking the assembling of ourselves together, as the manner of some is; but exhorting one another: and so much the more, as ye see the day approaching.

Hebrews 10:25

Exercise or Use Your Faith

Even so faith, if it hath not works, is dead, being alone.

James 2:17

When I became a Christian, I immediately believed that God is able to heal and that He is the greatest physician. God does not manage sickness, He takes them away from the root from our bodies. I asked myself, "How can I see this manifest in my life and in the lives of His people?" I began to pray for the sick and pray for myself whenever I was not well. By so doing, my faith developed greatly in the area of healing. I believe that God has granted us the grace to walk in divine healing as believers for by His stripes we were healed.

I remember once, a friend in my class said to me that he was having pains in his abdomen. This was the early stages of my Christian life, but by faith, I took him to the park and prayed for him. To my amazement, he was healed. This is how to exercise faith. You must use the word of God in situations that you find yourself in. As you use the word of God and it works for you, your faith increases and moves you to the next level of faith.

The word of God tells me that faith without works is a dead faith. From those humble beginnings, I now see cancer patients, people with fibroids, people who cannot walk people with high blood pressure and diverse kinds of diseases healed by Almighty God when I pray.

Another area that I also exercised my faith was by going for evangelism. I remember as a student, I would go alone and knock on the doors of fellow students and minister the word of God to them. By so doing, I led many to Christ in the university I attended. Unless you use your faith, you will never know what God can do through you. Exercise your faith and allow the Lord to manifest through you.

Praying in the Holy Ghost

But ye, beloved, building up yourselves on your most holy faith, praying in the Holy Ghost,

Jude 1:20

Prayer is another source of increasing your faith but it is not just any kind of prayer but the prayer in the Holy Ghost. **Jude** encourages us to build our faith by praying in tongues. I can speak in tongues for hours and as I do, my faith increases as the Holy Ghost stirs me up. When a rechargeable battery goes low, it is charged again by plugging it into an electrical socket. This gives life to the battery again.

A prayerless Christian is a faithless Christian. This is because, when you do not pray, you become very dry and distant from God. And in your dry state, your faith is very low. To the believer, speaking in tongues recharges you and imparts tremendous faith to you. As the word of God says in **1 Corinthians 14:4**, *"For he that speaks in an unknown tongue edifies himself* (or recharges himself)."

Stand Firm in your Faith

The Christian walk is all about faith and without faith we will not advance in the kingdom of God. True faith is Jesus Christ all other sources of faith are false. I pray that you will put your faith in Jesus who is the Author and Finisher of our faith. He is the beginning and the end of faith. I pray for you that your faith will continue to increase as you walk with the Lord.

I see your faith growing! I see your faith moving mountains! I see your faith crushing the head of the serpent! I see your faith overcoming every obstacle that comes your way! I see you standing firm in Christ because of your faith! In the mighty name of Jesus Christ.

Prayer of salvation

If you have read this book and you want to surrender your life to Jesus today, please say this simple prayer. Pray it from your heart, believe it and you shall be saved. Say this prayer loudly:

Dear Lord Jesus, I recognise that I am a sinner.

I recognise that You died for me and paid the penalty

for my sins.

Dear Lord Jesus, today I repent of my sins and I accept

You as my Lord and my Saviour.

Wash me with Your blood and make me holy.

Please write my name in the book of life and give me

the grace to serve You.

Thank you that I am born again.

AMEN

If you have said this prayer, you are now born again! You are now a new creation in Christ! Congratulations! I advise you to find a good Bible believing church where the solid word of God is taught and attend regularly. God bless you.

Other titles by Ernest Addo

THREE DIMENSIONS OF MAN

This book will enlighten you about your REAL self and how to live as a born again Christian. In it, you will discover:

- *The spirit of man and how to build it.*

- *The soul of man and how to transform it.*

- *The body of man and how to keep it under control.*

- *The significance of Water Baptism.*

- *How to strengthen your Christian life through God's Word, Prayer, Fellowship and much more.*

- *An index of useful scriptures to memorise.*

Written in a practical style, this book will teach you essential biblical principles and how to apply them step by step in your Christian walk. As you learn these foundational truths, you will be equipped to become a better Christian!